#33.00

YA 005.82
INT

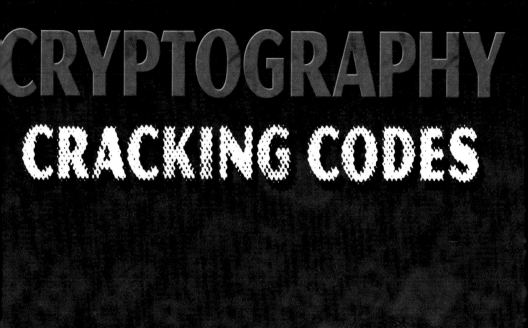

CRYPTOGRAPHY
CRACKING CODES

INTELLIGENCE and COUNTERINTELLIGENCE

CRYPTOGRAPHY
CRACKING CODES

EDITED BY ROB CURLEY, SENIOR EDITOR,
SCIENCE AND TECHNOLOGY

Britannica
— **Educational Publishing** —

IN ASSOCIATION WITH

ROSEN
EDUCATIONAL SERVICES

Published in 2013 by Britannica Educational Publishing
(a trademark of Encyclopædia Britannica, Inc.)
in association with Rosen Educational Services, LLC
29 East 21st Street, New York, NY 10010.

First Edition

Britannica Educational Publishing
Rob Curley: Senior Editor, Science and Technology
J.E. Luebering: Senior Manager
Adam Augustyn: Assistant Manager
Marilyn L. Barton: Senior Coordinator, Production Control
Steven Bosco: Director, Editorial Technologies
Lisa S. Braucher: Senior Producer and Data Editor
Yvette Charboneau: Senior Copy Editor
Kathy Nakamura: Manager, Media Acquisition

Rosen Educational Services
Nicholas Croce: Editor
Nelson Sá: Art Director
Cindy Reiman: Photography Manager
Karen Huang: Photo Researcher
Brian Garvey: Designer, Cover Design
Introduction by Richard Barrington

Library of Congress Cataloging-in-Publication Data

Intelligence and counterintelligence: cryptography: cracking codes/edited by Rob Curley.—
First edition.
   pages cm
"In association with Britannica Educational Publishing, Rosen Educational Services."
Includes bibliographical references and index.
ISBN 978-1-62275-034-4 (library binding)
1. Cryptography—History. 2. Data encryption (Computer science) I. Curley, Robert. II.
Title: Cryptography: cracking codes.
Z103.I68 2013
005.8'2—dc23

2012035291

Manufactured in the United States of America

On the cover, pp. i, iii: Binary code. *Comstock/Thinkstock*

Cover (top front and back) © www.iStockphoto.com/Yucel Yilmaz; ba ck cover © www.iStockphoto.com/Alexander Putyata; pp. 1, 15, 30, 41, 50, 63, 75, 77, 78 © www.iStockphoto.com/Olga Yakovenko; pp.12, 27, 28, 38, 43, 44, 59, 60, 67 © www.iStockphoto.com/Molnár Ákos

CONTENTS

Introduction   viii

**Chapter 1: Cryptography,
Cryptanalysis, and Cryptology**   1

    The Fundamentals of Codes,
    Ciphers, and Authentication   2

    Cryptology in Private and
    Commercial Life   8

    Identity Theft   12

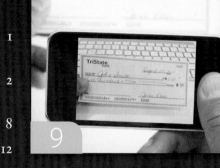

Chapter 2: Cipher Systems   15

    Transposition Ciphers   15

    Substitution Ciphers   17

        Playfair Ciphers   18

        Vigenère Ciphers   20

        Vernam-Vigenère Ciphers   24

    William and Elizebeth Friedman   27

    Product Ciphers   28

**Chapter 3: Key Systems and
Block and Stream Ciphers**   30

    Single-Key Cryptography   30

    Two-Key Cryptography   31

        Public-Key Cryptography   33

        Secret-Sharing   35

        RSA Encryption   36

    Prime Numbers   38

    Block and Stream Ciphers   39

42

57

Chapter 4: Cryptanalysis   41

Basic Aspects   42

The Zimmermann Telegram   43

Types of Cryptanalysis   46

Chapter 5: Early Manual and Mechanical Cryptography   50

The First Systems   51

World Wars I and II   54

Alan Turing's Bombe   59

Chapter 6: Modern Electronic Cryptography   63

The Impact of Electronics   64

Fibonacci's Numbers   67

DES and AES   68

Conclusion   74

Glossary   75

Bibliography   77

Index   78

INTRODUCTION

Binary code. Spaxiax/Shutterstock.com

The world of secret messages and code breakers might seem like something out of a high-tech espionage thriller, but the fascination we have with cryptology and its methods in novels has been inspired by some very real practices. At times, these practices have helped change history, and while cryptology continues to adapt by using cutting-edge technology, it is a science—and to some extent an art—with roots that go back to ancient times.

This book will let you in on the secrets of cryptography and code breaking, including their colourful history, the extremely intricate structures that go into cryptographic systems, and the high-level puzzle-solving required to break a code. In the process, you will see both sides of a cat-and-mouse game: those who are trying to devise impenetrable codes, and those who are trying to crack those codes.

Given the long history of the practice, it is appropriate that the word *cryptography* comes from ancient Greek. It literally means "hidden writing," and the practice is one of trying to conceal messages in plain sight. Cryptanalysis represents the other side of game: the practice of trying to decipher or forge messages written in someone else's code. Cryptology is a broad description of the overall field, encompassing both cryptography and cryptanalysis.

Talk of secret messages and code breakers evokes images of spies and international diplomacy, and cryptology continues to play its traditional role in that realm. However, in a world of electronic commerce, cryptology is also central to more mundane types of business, as each day it allows millions of financial transactions to take place with safety and ease.

Fundamentally, cryptography is based on a key, which is the formula for converting the original message (known as plaintext) into a cipher, or a secretly coded message. The process for making this conversion is known as encryption, and the reverse process is known as decryption.

The use of a key to convert information into a cipher can be quite simple, but there are various techniques for making that conversion process more complex, and thus the cipher harder to crack. This book will show how modern encryption methods have built on the basic principles of cryptography to create increasingly elaborate yet efficiently automated methods of securely encoding information.

These encryption methods are essential to 21st century electronic commerce. Credit and debit cards, Internet transactions, and electronic money transfers all rely on principles of cryptography. In addition to using cryptography to safeguard information belonging to consumers, merchants, and financial institutions, electronic commerce relies on cryptography for one other element that is necessary for automated transactions, and that is authentication. In a world where the parties to a transaction increasingly do not meet face to face, encrypted authentication methods are vital to ensuring that those parties are whom they claim to be.

Unfortunately, encryption methods have become increasingly sophisticated out of necessity, as the theft and unauthorised decryption of sensitive information has grown right along with electronic commerce itself. Illegal decryption is often the basis for cyber crimes such as identity theft. By the first decade of the 21st century, this type of fraud was already affecting millions of people in the United States alone, resulting in the losses of billions of dollars by businesses and consumers.

While encryption methods continue to evolve to meet the growing security challenge, a look back at the origins of cryptography provides some insight into the basic building blocks of today's systems. This book will examine the historical development of the two major types of ciphers: transpositions and substitutions. Transposition ciphers conceal a message by scrambling the sequence of its components, while substitution ciphers replace those components with different letters, numbers, or other symbols while maintaining the same sequence.

Transposition ciphers, which often use an agreed-upon keyword to signal the rearrangement of the letters in the original text, were popular in the early history of cryptography, and are still used today in more complex forms, which often entails layering one transposition on top of another to further scramble the message.

Substitution ciphers are the way codes have often been depicted in popular stories and films: a letter or symbol is substituted for each letter of the alphabet, and the original message is converted accordingly. In its simplest form, this has the drawback of presenting an often-recognisable pattern of how the characters appear, according to the language of the original text. To obscure those patterns, variations on substitution ciphers have been developed, such as using multiple alphabets so the substitution does not correlate as closely with the original message.

With both transposition and substitution ciphers, a key to avoiding unauthorised decoding of the message can be the level of complexity, as often one set of encryption rules is layered on top of another. This book will look at some significant examples of how this has been done. Historically, this effort has included variations on substitution ciphers such as Playfair ciphers, Vigenère ciphers, and Vernam-Vigenère ciphers. Product ciphers are cryptography systems employing multiple transpositions, and some ciphers have even employed a combination of substitution and transposition.

With each new level of complexity, cryptologists thought they had devised an unbreakable cipher—only to have resourceful code breakers prove them wrong. Because of the nature of this adversarial game, over the years cryptology developed a colourful history. The use of ciphers in wartime and in criminal activity, and the efforts to crack those ciphers, often had a dramatic impact.

Whether a cipher is simple or complex, at its heart is the key—the system for how the original information is coded into a cipher. Because the key is the basis for coding information, it is also the basis for decoding that information, which makes it a critical security concern. Distributing and protecting these keys is of such concern that in military operations, keys themselves may be disseminated in code, which must be decoded according to a different key before the coded key can be applied to a message. In business applications, a central problem is the sheer number of people exchanging coded information, which requires each pair in an exchange to have a unique code.

An important development in safeguarding the security of cipher keys was the creation of the two-key system, in which each user has a unique encryption and decryption key. This type of system is known as secret-sharing, because two or more people must participate in the decryption of a message. Secret-sharing is a central element in modern security procedures.

Another critical issue in two-key systems is authentication—verifying that a message came from the person it claims to be from. Thus, the method for coding information is just the beginning. Modern encryption and decryption systems also have to provide for communicating multiple keys and authenticating the identity of sender and recipient. In U.S. government security circles, all of this complexity results in key systems that are based on 310-digit numbers. To add yet another wrinkle, block ciphers and stream ciphers break information up into sections, each of which is coded using a different part of the encryption key. Thus, even if some of the message is decoded, the rest cannot be interpreted unless changes in the decryption key are perfectly synchronised with the encryption key.

Cryptologists haven't devised these elaborate systems simply out of a love of mathematical complexity. As cryptology has become more complex, it has been followed stride for stride by cryptanalysis, which is the unauthorised interpretation or forgery of encrypted information.

While cryptology is largely a question of scientifically structuring and layering encryption principles, cryptanalysis is often a combination of science and art, as flashes of inspiration can be just as important as quantitative analysis in cracking a code. Still, as codes become more complex, cryptanalysis relies more and more on computing power to discern patterns in the text, and longer passages of encrypted information may be necessary before those patterns can emerge.

This book will describe a variety of ways cryptanalysis is approached. A general principle is to be able to match a section of deciphered text with a section of cipher, in order to figure out the encryption principle and apply it to other sections of the cipher. This can be done if a portion of the text is known to the cryptanalyst or can be guessed at due to context. Another approach is to use computers to apply vast numbers of possible decryption principles to the cipher, until a passage appears that makes sense. Then, the decryption method applying to that passage can be applied to the rest of the cipher.

Cryptanalysis has some of the characteristics of a game, but in truth it is often very serious business. In this book, you'll see how code breaking played an important role in both world wars, and how it continues to be pursued intently by intelligence agencies around the world.

A recurring theme in this story of cryptology is the role of technology, and technology helps define three distinct eras in the history of cryptology. In the first phase, ciphers were constructed manually, and while new ciphers were devised all the time, the manual approach to implementing them was little changed for two thousand years, until just after World War I. At that point the mechanised era of cryptology began, starting first with calculating machines and progressing to the use of rotor machines by all participants in World War II. These machines could encrypt and decrypt faster than any manual operation and with less chance of error. The third era of cryptology came in the late 20th century with the switch to advanced computers, which can process trillions of bits of cipher in a matter of seconds. The third era of cryptology involves not so much the method of constructing ciphers as it does the massive deployment of them to a vastly expanded range of applications in the information age.

Some examples of the first two of these eras help illustrate the ongoing role that cryptology has played in the history of civilisation. Beginning with the use of ciphers by Spartan military commanders around the year 400 BCE, this book will show how cryptology has been applied down through time. Though the dawn of the mechanised era of cryptology in the 20th century increased the complexity of ciphers that could be implemented, it is fascinating to see how some of the basic principles of cryptology that date back hundreds of years or more remain in place to this day.

Still, while cryptologists from ancient Greece or medieval Europe might understand the conceptual foundation of today's ciphers, they would be mystified by the enormous amount of computing power that is brought to bear to implement those ciphers. On the other side of the fence, a similar degree of computing muscle is applied to trying to crack those codes. The last section of this book will show how computers have shaped the evolution of modern cryptography.

Early computers were applied to cryptology shortly after World War II. At first, these were just electronic versions of earlier rotor cipher machines, which were a mechanical means of varying a cipher key periodically to increase the complexity of the overall cipher. The potential of computers to radically change the game was realised slowly — in fact, those mechanical rotor machines were still used simultaneously with computers up until the 1980s.

Encryption techniques began to fully take advantage of computing power with the adoption of the Data Encryption Standard (DES) by the United States in the mid-1970s. Under this standard, an ever-changing sequence of 16 rounds of substitutions and transpositions are layered on top of one another to create a cipher whose complexity would be well beyond any mechanical means of construction. The DES became the international financial and business standard for encryption.

However, just as computing power increased the complexity of encryption, it also advanced the speed with which information could be analysed and decrypted. By the late 1990s, it was apparent that even DES ciphers were vulnerable to this type of cryptanalysis. So, in 2000 a new encryption standard was approved, the Advanced Encryption Standard (AES). The AES not only took advantage of advances in computer hardware and software since the DES had been formulated, but it was also designed to be adaptable by increasing its key length if conditions call for it.

Will the AES prove to be the ultimate move in the cat-and-mouse game between cryptographers and cryptanalysts? It remains to be seen, but given what's at stake in both international affairs and electronic commerce, one thing is certain: that secret game will continue.

The clandestine world this book explores was once the territory of spies and diplomats. Today, electronic commerce has made cryptography an essential element of everyday life. By learning about how cryptography works, its various applications in the modern world, and the threats to its protections, you can better appreciate how these methods affect you, and perhaps learn how to more effectively safeguard your information.

CHAPTER 1

CRYPTOGRAPHY, CRYPTANALYSIS, AND CRYPTOLOGY

The term *cryptography* is derived from the Greek *kryptós* ("hidden") and *gráphein*, ("to write"). Cryptography was originally the study of the principles and techniques by which information could be concealed in ciphers and later revealed by legitimate users employing the secret key. It now encompasses the whole area of key-controlled transformations of information into forms that are either impossible or computationally infeasible for unauthorized persons to duplicate or undo.

Cryptanalysis (from the Greek *kryptós* and *analýein*, "to loosen" or "to untie") is the science and art of recovering or forging cryptographically secured information without knowledge of the key. Cryptology (from the Greek *kryptós* and *lógos*, "word") is often—and mistakenly—considered a synonym for cryptography and occasionally for cryptanalysis, but specialists in the field have for years adopted the convention that cryptology is the more inclusive term, encompassing both cryptography and cryptanalysis and including the entire science concerned with data communication and storage in secure and usually secret form.

Cryptography was initially concerned only with providing secrecy for written messages, especially in times of war. Its principles apply equally well, however, to securing data flowing between computers or data stored in them, to encrypting facsimile and television signals, to verifying the identity of participants in e-commerce, and providing legally acceptable records of those transactions. Because of this broadened interpretation of cryptography, the field of cryptanalysis has also been enlarged.

THE FUNDAMENTALS OF CODES, CIPHERS, AND AUTHENTICATION

Security is obtained from legitimate users being able to transform information by virtue of a secret key or keys — i.e., information known only to them. The resulting cipher, although generally inscrutable and not forgeable without the secret key, can be decrypted by anyone knowing the key either to recover the hidden information or to authenticate the source. Secrecy, though still an important function in cryptology, is often no longer the main purpose of using a transformation, and the resulting transformation may be only loosely considered a cipher.

Because much of the terminology of cryptology dates to a time when written messages were the only things being secured, the source information, even if it is an apparently incomprehensible binary stream of 1s and 0s, as in computer output, is referred to as the plaintext. As noted above, the secret information known only to the legitimate users is the key, and the transformation of the plaintext under the control of the key into a cipher (also called ciphertext) is referred to as encryption. The inverse operation, by which a legitimate receiver recovers the concealed information from the cipher using the key, is known as decryption.

The most frequently confused, and misused, terms in the lexicon of cryptology are *code* and *cipher*. Even experts occasionally employ these terms as though they were synonymous.

MORSE CODE

A ● ━		Period . ● ━ ● ━ ● ━	
B ━ ● ● ●		Comma , ━ ━ ● ● ━ ━	
C ━ ● ━ ●		Question mark ? ● ● ━ ━ ● ●	
D ━ ● ●		Apostrophe ' ● ━ ━ ━ ━ ●	
E ●		Exclamation mark ! ━ ● ━ ● ━ ━	
F ● ● ━ ●		Slash, Fraction bar / ━ ● ● ━ ●	
G ━ ━ ●		Parenthesis open (━ ● ━ ━ ●	
H ● ● ● ●		Parenthesis closed) ━ ● ━ ━ ● ━	
I ● ●		Ampersand, Wait & ● ━ ● ● ●	
J ● ━ ━ ━		Colon : ━ ━ ━ ● ● ●	
K ━ ● ━		Semicolon ; ━ ● ━ ● ━ ●	
L ● ━ ● ●		Double dash = ━ ● ● ● ━	
M ━ ━		Plus + ● ━ ● ━ ●	
N ━ ●		Hyphen, Minus - ━ ● ● ● ● ━	
O ━ ━ ━		Underscore _ ● ● ━ ━ ● ━	
P ● ━ ━ ●		Quotation mark " ● ━ ● ● ━ ●	
Q ━ ━ ● ━		Dollar sign $ ● ● ● ━ ● ● ━	
R ● ━ ●		At sign @ ● ━ ━ ● ━ ●	
S ● ● ●			
T ━			
U ● ● ━			
V ● ● ● ━	1 ● ━ ━ ━ ━	6 ━ ● ● ● ●
W ● ━ ━	2 ● ● ━ ━ ━	7 ━ ━ ● ● ●
X ━ ● ● ━	3 ● ● ● ━ ━	8 ━ ━ ━ ● ●
Y ━ ● ━ ━	4 ● ● ● ● ━	9 ━ ━ ━ ━ ●
Z ━ ━ ● ●	5 ● ● ● ● ●	0 ━ ━ ━ ━ ━

Morse code. Laralova/Shutterstock.com

A code is simply an unvarying rule for replacing a piece of information (e.g., letter, word, or phrase) with another object, but not necessarily of the same sort; Morse code, which replaces alphanumeric characters with patterns of dots and dashes, is a familiar example. Probably the most widely known code in use today is the American Standard Code for Information Interchange (ASCII). Employed in all personal computers and terminals, it represents 128 characters (and operations such as backspace and carriage

3

return) in the form of seven-bit binary numbers—i.e., as a string of seven 1s and 0s. In ASCII a lowercase a is always 1100001, an uppercase A always 1000001, and so on. Acronyms are also widely known and used codes, as, for example, FAQ (for "frequently asked question") and COD (meaning "cash on delivery"). Occasionally such a code word achieves an independent existence (and meaning) while the original equivalent phrase is forgotten or at least no longer has the precise meaning attributed to the code word—e.g., modem (originally standing for "modulator-demodulator").

Ciphers, as in the case of codes, also replace a piece of information (an element of the plaintext that may consist of a letter, word, or string of symbols) with another object. The difference is that the replacement is made according to a rule defined by a secret key known only to the transmitter and legitimate receiver in the expectation that an outsider, ignorant of the key, will not be able to invert the replacement to decrypt the cipher. In the past, the blurring of the distinction between codes and ciphers was relatively unimportant. In contemporary communications, however, information is frequently both encoded and encrypted so that it is important to understand the difference. A satellite communications link, for example, may encode information in ASCII characters if it is textual, or pulse-code modulate and digitize it in binary-coded decimal (BCD) form if it is an analog signal such as speech. The resulting coded data is then encrypted into ciphers by using the Data Encryption Standard or the Advanced Encryption Standard (DES or AES; described in the chapter "Modern Electronic Cryptography"). Finally, the resulting cipher stream itself is encoded again, using error-correcting codes for transmission from the ground station to the orbiting satellite and thence back to another ground station. These operations are then undone, in reverse order, by the intended receiver to recover the original information.

In the simplest possible example of a true cipher, A wishes to send one of two equally likely messages to B, say, to buy or sell a particular stock. The communication must take place over a wireless telephone on which eavesdroppers may listen in. It is vital to A's and B's interests that others not be privy to the content of their communication. In order to foil any eavesdroppers, A and B agree in advance as to whether A will actually say what he wishes B to do, or the opposite. Because this decision on their part must be unpredictable, they decide by flipping a coin. If heads comes up, A will say *Buy* when he wants B to buy and *Sell* when he wants B to sell. If tails comes up, however, he will say *Buy* when he wants B to sell, and so forth. (The messages communicate only one bit of information and could therefore be 1 and 0, but the example is clearer using *Buy* and *Sell*.)

		plaintext	
		Buy	Sell
key	H	Buy	Sell
	T	Sell	Buy

With this encryption/decryption protocol being used, an eavesdropper gains no knowledge about the actual (concealed) instruction A has sent to B as a result of listening to their telephone communication. Such a cryptosystem is defined as "perfect." The key in this simple example is the knowledge (shared by A and B) of whether A is saying what he wishes B to do or the opposite. Encryption is the act by A of either saying what he wants done or not as determined by the key, while decryption is the interpretation by B of what A actually meant, not necessarily of what he said.

This example can be extended to illustrate the second basic function of cryptography, providing a means for B to assure himself that an instruction has actually come from A and that it is unaltered—i.e., a means of authenticating the message. In the example, if the eavesdropper intercepted A's message to B, he could—even without knowing the prearranged key—cause B to act contrary to A's intent by passing along to B the opposite of what A sent. Similarly, he could simply impersonate A and tell B to buy or sell without waiting for A to send a message, although he would not know in advance which action B would take as a result. In either event, the eavesdropper would be certain of deceiving B into doing something that A had not requested.

To protect against this sort of deception by outsiders, A and B could use the following encryption/decryption protocol.

plaintext

		Buy	Sell
	HH	Buy-1	Sell-1
	HT	Buy-0	Sell-0
key	TH	Sell-1	Buy-0
	TT	Sell-0	Buy-1

They secretly flip a coin twice to choose one of four equally likely keys, labeled HH, HT, TH, and TT, with both of them knowing which key has been chosen. The outcome of the first coin flip determines the encryption rule just as in the previous example. The two coin flips together determine an authentication bit, 0 or 1, to be appended to the ciphers to form four possible messages: Buy-1, Buy-0, Sell-1, and Sell-0. B will only accept a message as authentic if it occurs in the row corresponding to the secret key. The pair of messages not in that row will be rejected by B as non-authentic. B can easily interpret the cipher in an authentic message to recover A's instructions using the outcome of the first coin flip as the key. If a third party C impersonates A and sends a message without waiting for A to do so, he will, with probability $1/2$, choose a message that does not occur in the row corresponding to the key A and B are using. Hence, the attempted deception will be detected by B, with probability $1/2$. If C waits and intercepts a message from A, no matter which message it is, he will be faced with a choice between two equally likely keys that A and B could be using. As in the previous example, the two messages he must choose between convey different instructions to B, but now one of the ciphers has a 1 and the other a 0 appended as the authentication bit, and only one of these will be accepted by B. Consequently, C's chances of deceiving B into acting contrary to A's instructions are still $1/2$; namely, eavesdropping on A and B's conversation has not improved C's chances of deceiving B.

Clearly in either example, secrecy or secrecy with authentication, the same key cannot be reused. If C learned the message by eavesdropping and observed B's response, he could deduce the key and thereafter impersonate A with certainty of success. If, however, A and B chose as many random keys as they had messages to exchange, the security of the information would remain the same for all exchanges. When used in this manner, these examples illustrate the vital concept of a onetime key, which is the basis for the only cryptosystems that can be mathematically proved to be cryptosecure. This may seem like a "toy" example, but it illustrates the essential features of cryptography. It is worth remarking that the first example shows how even a child can create ciphers, at a cost of making as many flips of a fair coin as he has bits of information to conceal, that cannot be "broken" by even national cryptologic services with arbitrary computing power—disabusing the lay notion that the unachieved goal of cryptography is to devise a cipher that cannot be broken.

CRYPTOLOGY IN PRIVATE AND COMMERCIAL LIFE

At the very end of the 20th century, a revolution occurred in the way private citizens and businesses made use of and were dependent on pure information, i.e., information with no meaningful physical embodiment. This was sparked by two technical developments: an almost universal access to affordable real-time global communications, and the practical capability to acquire, process, store, and disseminate virtually unlimited amounts of information. Electronic banking, personal computers, the Internet and associated e-commerce, and "smart" cards were some of the more obvious instances where this revolution affected every aspect of private and commercial life.

To appreciate how this involved cryptology, contrast what is involved when a customer makes a noncash purchase in person with what is involved in a similar transaction in e-commerce. For a direct purchase, the merchant routinely asks for some photo identification, usually a driver's license, to verify the customer's identity. Neither party is ordinarily concerned with secrecy; both are vitally concerned with other aspects of information integrity. Next, consider an analogous transaction over the

Many banks allow customers to deposit checks simply by taking a picture of it with a smartphone app. Vstock LLC/Getty Images

Internet. The merchant must still verify the customer's identity, even though they may be separated by thousands of miles, and the customer must still be assured that he will only be charged the agreed amount. However, there is a whole gamut of new concerns. The customer must be assured that information he communicates to the merchant is confidential and protected from interception by others. And while the merchant retains the customer's signature as material proof of a direct transaction, he has only a string of 0s and 1s on a hard disk following an e-commerce transaction. The merchant must be confident that this "information" will suffice for him to collect payment, as well as protect him should the customer later disavow the transaction or claim that it was for a different amount. All of these concerns, and more, have to be met before the simplest e-commerce transactions can be made securely. As a result, cryptology has been extended far beyond its original function of providing secrecy.

The conduct of commerce, affairs of state, military actions, and personal affairs all depend on the existence of generally accepted means of authenticating identity, authority, ownership, license, signature, notarization, date of action, receipt, and so on. In the past these have depended almost entirely on documents, and on protocols for the creation of those documents, for authentication. Society has evolved and adopted a complex set of legal and forensic procedures, depending almost entirely on the physical evidence intrinsic to the documents themselves, to resolve disputes over authenticity. In the information age, however, possession, control, transfer, or access to real assets is frequently based on electronic information, and a license to use, modify, or disseminate valuable information itself is similarly determined. Thus, it is essential that internal evidence be present in the information itself—since that is the only thing available. Modern cryptology, therefore, must provide every function presently served by documents—public and private. In fact, it frequently must do more. When someone mails a document by certified mail with a request for a delivery receipt, the receipt only proves that an envelope was delivered; it says nothing about the contents. Digital certificates of origination and digital receipts, though, are inextricably linked to each electronic document. Many other functions, such as signatures, are also much more demanding in a digital setting. In June 2000 the U.S. Congress gave digital signatures the same legal status as written signatures—the first such legislation in the world.

In classical cryptology the participants trust each other but not outsiders; typical examples include diplomatic communications and military commands. In business and personal transactions, though, the situation is almost the opposite, as the participants may have various motives for cheating. For example, the cheater may wish to impersonate some other participant, to eavesdrop on communications between other participants, or to intercept and modify information being communicated between other users. The cheater may be an insider who wishes to disavow communications he actually originated or to claim to have received messages from other participants who did not send them. He may wish to enlarge his license to gain access to information to which he is not supposed to have access or to alter the license of others. He may wish simply to subvert the system to deny services to others or to cause other users to reject as fraudulent information that is in fact legitimate. Therefore, modern cryptology must also prevent every form of cheating or, failing that, detect cheating in information-based systems where the means for cheating depends only on tampering with electronic information.

At the beginning of the 1990s most people would have been hard-pressed to say where cryptology had an impact on their day-to-day lives. Today, people who have purchased merchandise over the Internet are familiar with warnings that they are about to exchange information over a secure link. When a warning appears from time to time alerting consumers that a merchant's authentication has either expired or is not working, they are aware that this is a warning to proceed at their own risk in providing personal information, such as credit card numbers. Only a few are aware, however, that behind this exchange of authentications is a 128-bit cryptography key that has been

IDENTITY THEFT

In the United States, individuals do not have an official identity card but a Social Security number that has long served as a de facto identification number. Taxes are collected on the basis of each citizen's Social Security number, and many private institutions use the number to keep track of their employees, students, and patients. Access to an individual's Social Security number affords the opportunity to gather all the documents related to that person's citizenship—i.e., to steal his identity.

Even stolen credit card information can be used to reconstruct an individual's identity. When criminals steal a firm's credit card records, they produce two distinct effects. First, they make off with digital information about individuals that is useful in many ways. For example, they might use the credit card information to run up huge bills, forcing the credit card firms to suffer large losses, or they might sell the information to others who can use it in a similar fashion. Second, they might use individual credit card names and numbers to create new identities for other criminals. For example, a criminal might contact the issuing bank of a stolen credit card and change the mailing address on the account. Next, the criminal may get a passport or driver's license with his own picture but with the victim's name. With a driver's license, the criminal can easily acquire a new Social Security card; it is then possible to open bank accounts and receive loans—all with the victim's credit record and background. The original cardholder might remain unaware of this until the debt is so great that the bank contacts the account holder. Only then does the identity theft become visible.

in common use around the world for transactions over the Internet since it was approved for export by the U.S. government in 2000, replacing an earlier 40-bit key that had been made insecure by the growing power of computers to test it. The 128-bit key offers "strong encryption" that protects Internet transactions against almost any threat; nevertheless, some Web browsers used on personal computers will support an even stronger 256-bit encryption key, which offers a level of protection required by many governments for top-secret documents.

Cryptology, indeed, has long been a part of modern daily life. In particular, electronic banking and various financial, medical, and legal databases depend on cryptology for security. One example is the personal identity number (PIN), a coded identification that must be entered into an automated teller machine (ATM) along with a bankcard to corroborate that the card is being used by an authorized bearer. The PIN may be stored in an encrypted form (as a cipher) either in the bank's computers or on the card itself. The transformation used in this type of cryptography is called one-way; i.e., it is easy to compute a cipher given the bank's key and the customer's PIN, but it is computationally infeasible to compute the plaintext PIN from the cipher even when the key is known. This protects the cardholder from being impersonated by someone who has access to the bank's computer files. Similarly, communications between the ATM and the bank's central computer are encrypted to prevent a would-be thief from tapping into the phone lines and recording the signals sent to the ATM to authorize the dispensing of cash in response to a legitimate user request and then later feeding the same signals to the ATM repeatedly to deceive it into dispensing money illegitimately from the customer's account.

A novel application that involves all aspects of cryptography is the "smart" credit card, which has a microprocessor built into the card itself. The user must corroborate his identity to the card each time a transaction is made in much the same way that a PIN is used with an ATM. The card and the card reader execute a sequence of encrypted sign/countersign-like exchanges to verify that each is dealing with a legitimate counterpart. Once this has been established, the transaction itself is carried out in encrypted form to prevent anyone, including the cardholder or the merchant whose card reader is involved, from eavesdropping on the exchange and then later impersonating either party to defraud the system. This elaborate protocol is carried out in a way that is invisible to the user, except for the necessity of entering a PIN to initiate the transaction. Smart cards are in widespread use throughout Europe, much more so than the "dumb" plastic cards common in the United States. The Advanced Encryption Standard (AES), approved as a secure communications standard by the U.S. National Institute of Standards and Technology (NIST) in 2000, is compatible with implementation in smart cards, unlike its predecessor, the Data Encryption Standard (DES).

CHAPTER 2

CIPHER SYSTEMS

Cryptography, as defined previously, is the science of transforming information into a form that is impossible or infeasible to duplicate or undo without knowledge of a secret key. The easiest way to describe the techniques on which cryptography depends is first to examine some simple cipher systems and then abstract from these examples features that apply to more complex systems. There are two basic kinds of mathematical operations used in cipher systems: transpositions and substitutions. Transpositions rearrange the symbols in the plaintext without changing the symbols themselves. Substitutions replace plaintext elements (symbols, pairs of symbols, etc.) with other symbols or groups of symbols without changing the sequence in which they occur.

TRANSPOSITION CIPHERS

In manual systems transpositions are generally carried out with the aid of an easily remembered mnemonic. For example, a popular schoolboy cipher is the "rail fence," in which letters of the plaintext are written alternating between rows and the rows are then read sequentially to give the cipher. In a depth-two rail fence (two rows) the message WE ARE DISCOVERED SAVE YOURSELF would be written

```
W A E I C V R D A E O R E F
E R D S O E E S V Y U S L
```

or

```
W A E I C V R D A E O R E F E R D S O E E S V Y U S L .
```

Simple frequency counts on the ciphertext would reveal to the cryptanalyst that letters occur with precisely the same frequency in the cipher as in an average plaintext and, hence, that a simple rearrangement of the letters is probable.

The rail fence is the simplest example of a class of transposition ciphers, known as route ciphers, that enjoyed considerable popularity in the early history of cryptology. In general, the elements of the plaintext (usually single letters) are written in a prearranged order (route) into a geometric array (matrix)—typically a rectangle—agreed upon in advance by the transmitter and receiver and then read off by following another prescribed route through the matrix to produce the cipher. The key in a route cipher consists of keeping secret the geometric array, the starting point, and the routes. Clearly both the matrix and the routes can be much more complex than in this example; but even so, they provide little security. One form of transposition (permutation) that was widely used depends on an easily remembered key word for identifying the route in which the columns of a rectangular matrix are to be read. For example, using the key word AUTHOR and ordering the columns by the lexicographic order of the letters in the key word

```
A  U  T  H  O  R
1  6  5  2  3  4
-------------------
W  E  A  R  E  D
I  S  C  O  V  E
R  E  D  S  A  V
E  Y  O  U  R  S
E  L  F  A  B  C
```

yields the cipher

```
W I R E E R O S U A E V A R B D E V S C A C D O F E S E Y L .
```

16

In decrypting a route cipher, the receiver enters the ciphertext symbols into the agreed-upon matrix according to the encryption route and then reads the plaintext according to the original order of entry. A significant improvement in cryptosecurity can be achieved by reencrypting the cipher obtained from one transposition with another transposition. Because the result (product) of two transpositions is also a transposition, the effect of multiple transpositions is to define a complex route in the matrix, which in itself would be difficult to describe by any simple mnemonic. (*See* "Product Ciphers," later in this chapter.)

In the same class also fall systems that make use of perforated cardboard matrices called grilles; descriptions of such systems can be found in most older books on cryptography. In contemporary cryptography, transpositions serve principally as one of several encryption steps in forming a compound or product cipher.

SUBSTITUTION CIPHERS

In substitution ciphers, units of the plaintext (generally single letters or pairs of letters) are replaced with other symbols or groups of symbols, which need not be the same as those used in the plaintext. For instance, in Sir Arthur Conan Doyle's *Adventure of the Dancing Men* (1903), Sherlock Holmes solves a monoalphabetic substitution cipher in which the ciphertext symbols are stick figures of a human in various dancelike poses.

The simplest of all substitution ciphers are those in which the cipher alphabet is merely a cyclical shift of the plaintext alphabet. Of these, the best-known is the Caesar cipher, used by Julius Caesar, in which A is encrypted as D, B as E, and so forth. As many a school-boy has discovered to his embarrassment, cyclical-shift substitution ciphers are not secure. And as is pointed out in the section "Cryptanalysis," neither is any other monoalphabetic substitution cipher in which a given plaintext symbol is always encrypted into the same ciphertext symbol. Because of the redundancy of the English language, only about 25 symbols of ciphertext are required to permit the cryptanalysis of monoalphabetic substitution ciphers, which makes them a popular source for recreational cryptograms. The explanation for this weakness is that the frequency distributions of symbols in the plaintext and in the ciphertext are identical, only the symbols having been relabeled. In fact, any structure or pattern in the plaintext is preserved intact in the ciphertext, so that the cryptanalyst's task is an easy one.

There are two main approaches that have been employed with substitution ciphers to lessen the extent to which structure in the plaintext—primarily single-letter frequencies—survives in the ciphertext. One approach is to encrypt elements of plaintext consisting of two or more symbols; e.g., digraphs and trigraphs. The other is to use several cipher alphabets. When this approach of polyalphabetic substitution is carried to its limit, it results in onetime keys, or pads.

PLAYFAIR CIPHERS

In cryptosystems for manually encrypting units of plaintext made up of more than a single letter, only digraphs were ever used. By treating digraphs in the plaintext as units rather than as single letters, the extent to which the raw frequency distribution survives the encryption process can be lessened but not eliminated, as letter pairs are themselves highly correlated. The best-known digraph substitution cipher is the Playfair, invented by Sir Charles Wheatstone but championed at the British Foreign Office by Lyon Playfair, the first Baron Playfair of St. Andrews. Below is an example of a Playfair cipher, solved by Lord Peter Wimsey in Dorothy L. Sayers's *Have His Carcase* (1932). Here, the mnemonic aid used to carry out the encryption is a 5 × 5-square matrix containing the letters of the alphabet (I and J are treated as the same letter). A key word, MONARCHY in this example, is filled in first, and the remaining unused letters of the alphabet are entered in their lexicographic order:

M	O	N	A	R
C	H	Y	B	D
E	F	G	I/J	K
L	P	Q	S	T
U	V	W	X	Z

Plaintext digraphs are encrypted with the matrix by first locating the two plaintext letters in the matrix. They are (1) in different rows and columns; (2) in the same row; (3) in the same column; or (4) alike. The corresponding encryption (replacement) rules are the following:

- When the two letters are in different rows and columns, each is replaced by the letter that is in the same row but in the other column; i.e., to encrypt WE, W is replaced by U and E by G.

- When A and R are in the same row, A is encrypted as R and R (reading the row cyclically) as M.
- When I and S are in the same column, I is encrypted as S and S as X.
- When a double letter occurs, a spurious symbol, say Q, is introduced so that the MM in SUMMER is encrypted as NL for MQ and CL for ME.
- An X is appended to the end of the plaintext if necessary to give the plaintext an even number of letters.

Encrypting the familiar plaintext example using Sayers's Playfair array yields:

```
Plaintext: WE ARE DISCOVERED SAVE YOURSELFX
Cipher:    UG RMK CSXHMUFMKB TOXG CMVATLUIV
```

If the frequency distribution information were totally concealed in the encryption process, the ciphertext plot of letter frequencies in Playfair ciphers would be flat. It is not. The deviation from this ideal is a measure of the tendency of some letter pairs to occur more frequently than others and of the Playfair's row-and-column correlation of symbols in the ciphertext—the essential structure exploited by a cryptanalyst in solving Playfair ciphers. The loss of a significant part of the plaintext frequency distribution, however, makes a Playfair cipher harder to cryptanalyze than a monoalphabetic cipher.

VIGENÈRE CIPHERS

The other approach to concealing plaintext structure in the ciphertext involves using several different monoalphabetic substitution ciphers rather than just one; the key specifies which particular substitution is to be employed for encrypting each plaintext symbol. The resulting ciphers, known generically as polyalphabetics, have a long history of usage. The systems differ mainly in the way in which the key is used to choose among the collection of monoalphabetic substitution rules.

The best-known polyalphabetics are the simple Vigenère ciphers, named for the 16th-century French cryptographer Blaise de Vigenère. For many years this type of cipher was thought to be impregnable and was known as *le chiffre indéchiffrable*, literally "the unbreakable cipher." The procedure for encrypting and decrypting Vigenère ciphers is illustrated in the figure.

```
  A B C D E F G H I J K L M N O P Q R S T U V W X Y Z

A A B C D E F G H I J K L M N O P Q R S T U V W X Y Z
B B C D E F G H I J K L M N O P Q R S T U V W X Y Z A
C C D E F G H I J K L M N O P Q R S T U V W X Y Z A B
D D E F G H I J K L M N O P Q R S T U V W X Y Z A B C
E E F G H I J K L M N O P Q R S T U V W X Y Z A B C D
F F G H I J K L M N O P Q R S T U V W X Y Z A B C D E
G G H I J K L M N O P Q R S T U V W X Y Z A B C D E F
H H I J K L M N O P Q R S T U V W X Y Z A B C D E F G
I I J K L M N O P Q R S T U V W X Y Z A B C D E F G H
J J K L M N O P Q R S T U V W X Y Z A B C D E F G H I
K K L M N O P Q R S T U V W X Y Z A B C D E F G H I J
L L M N O P Q R S T U V W X Y Z A B C D E F G H I J K
M M N O P Q R S T U V W X Y Z A B C D E F G H I J K L
N N O P Q R S T U V W X Y Z A B C D E F G H I J K L M
O O P Q R S T U V W X Y Z A B C D E F G H I J K L M N
P P Q R S T U V W X Y Z A B C D E F G H I J K L M N O
Q Q R S T U V W X Y Z A B C D E F G H I J K L M N O P
R R S T U V W X Y Z A B C D E F G H I J K L M N O P Q
S S T U V W X Y Z A B C D E F G H I J K L M N O P Q R
T T U V W X Y Z A B C D E F G H I J K L M N O P Q R S
U U V W X Y Z A B C D E F G H I J K L M N O P Q R S T
V V W X Y Z A B C D E F G H I J K L M N O P Q R S T U
W W X Y Z A B C D E F G H I J K L M N O P Q R S T U V
X X Y Z A B C D E F G H I J K L M N O P Q R S T U V W
Y Y Z A B C D E F G H I J K L M N O P Q R S T U V W X
Z Z A B C D E F G H I J K L M N O P Q R S T U V W X Y
```

In encrypting plaintext, the cipher letter is found at the intersection of the column headed by the plaintext letter and the row indexed by the key letter. To decrypt ciphertext, the plaintext letter is found at the head of the column determined by the intersection of the diagonal containing the cipher letter and the row containing the key letter. Encyclopædia Britannica, Inc.

cipher	VVVRBACP
key	COVERCOVER...
plaintext	THANKYOU

In the simplest systems of the Vigenère type, the key is a word or phrase that is repeated as many times as required to encipher a message. If the key is DECEPTIVE and the message is WE ARE DISCOVERED SAVE YOURSELF, then the resulting cipher will be

```
Message: WE ARE DISCOVERED SAVE YOURSELF
Key:     DE CEP TIVEDECEPT IVED ECEPTIVE
Cipher:  ZI CVT WQNGRZGVTW AVZH CQYGLMGJ.
```

In 1861 Friedrich W. Kasiski, formerly a German army officer and cryptanalyst, published a solution of repeated-key Vigenère ciphers based on the fact that identical pairings of message and key symbols generate the same cipher symbols. Cryptanalysts look for precisely such repetitions. In the example given above, the group VTW appears twice, separated by six letters, suggesting that the key (i.e., word) length is either three or nine. Consequently, the cryptanalyst would partition the cipher symbols into three and nine monoalphabets and attempt to solve each of these as a simple substitution cipher. With sufficient ciphertext, it would be easy to solve for the unknown key word.

The periodicity of a repeating key exploited by Kasiski can be eliminated by means of a running-key Vigenère cipher. Such a cipher is produced when a nonrepeating text is used for the key. Vigenère actually proposed concatenating the plaintext itself to follow a secret key word in order to provide a running key in what is known as an autokey.

Even though running-key or autokey ciphers eliminate periodicity, two methods exist to cryptanalyze them. In one, the cryptanalyst proceeds under the assumption that both the ciphertext and the key share the same frequency distribution of symbols and applies statistical analysis. For example, E occurs in English plaintext with a frequency of 0.0169, and T occurs only half as often. The cryptanalyst would, of course, need a much larger segment of ciphertext to solve a running-key Vigenère cipher, but the basic principle is essentially the same as before—i.e., the recurrence of like events yields identical effects in the ciphertext. The second method of solving running-key ciphers is commonly known as the probable-word method. In this approach, words that are thought most likely to occur in the text are subtracted from the cipher. For example, suppose that an encrypted message to President Jefferson Davis of the Confederate States of America was intercepted. Based on a statistical analysis of the letter frequencies in the ciphertext, and the South's encryption habits, it appears to employ a running-key Vigenère cipher. A reasonable choice for a probable word in the plaintext might be "PRESIDENT." For simplicity a space will be encoded as a "0." PRESIDENT would then be encoded—not encrypted—as "16, 18, 5, 19, 9, 4, 5, 14, 20" using the rule A = 1, B = 2, and so forth. Now these nine numbers are added modulo 27 (for the 26 letters plus a space symbol) to each successive block of nine symbols of ciphertext—shifting one letter each time to form a new block. Almost all such additions will produce random-like groups of nine symbols as a result, but some may produce a block that contains meaningful English fragments. These fragments can then be extended with either of the two techniques described above. If provided with enough ciphertext, the cryptanalyst can ultimately decrypt the cipher. What is important to bear in mind here is that the redundancy of the English language is high enough that the amount of information conveyed by every ciphertext component is greater than the rate at which equivocation (i.e., the uncertainty about the plaintext that the cryptanalyst must resolve to cryptanalyze the cipher) is introduced by the running key. In principle, when the

teletypewriter to decrypt the cipher. Vernam initially believed that a short random key could safely be reused many times, thus justifying the effort to deliver such a large key, but reuse of the key turned out to be vulnerable to attack by methods of the type devised by Kasiski. Vernam offered an alternative solution: a key generated by combining two shorter key tapes of m and n binary digits, or bits, where m and n share no common factor other than 1 (they are relatively prime). A bit stream so computed does not repeat until mn bits of key have been produced.

This version of the Vernam cipher system was adopted and employed by the U.S. Army until Major Joseph O. Mauborgne of the Army Signal Corps demonstrated during World War I that a cipher constructed from a key produced by linearly combining two or more short tapes could be decrypted by methods of the sort employed to cryptanalyze running-key ciphers. Mauborgne's work led to the realization that neither the repeating single-key nor the two-tape Vernam-Vigenère cipher system was cryptosecure. Of far greater consequence to modern cryptology—in fact, an idea that remains its cornerstone—was the conclusion drawn by Mauborgne and William F. Friedman that the only type of cryptosystem that is unconditionally secure uses a random onetime key. The proof of this, however, was provided almost 30 years later by another AT&T researcher, Claude Shannon, the father of modern information theory.

In a streaming cipher the key is incoherent—i.e., the uncertainty that the cryptanalyst has about each successive key symbol must be no less than the average information content of a message symbol. In a long "message" such as this book, the raw frequency of occurrence pattern is lost when the text is encrypted with a random onetime key, as indicated by the dotted curve in the following figure.

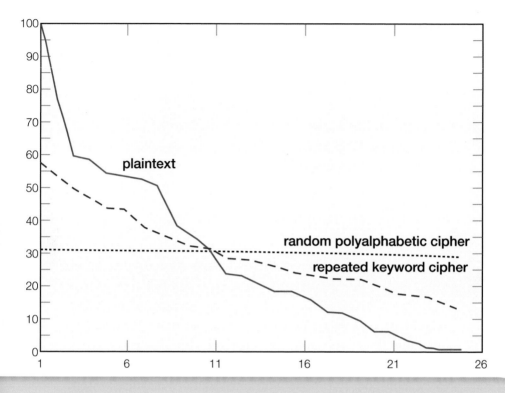

The most frequent plaintext letter is assigned a value of 100 and the remaining plaintext and ciphertext letters are given values from 0 to 100 relative to their frequency of occurrence. Thus, the most frequent letter (1 on the horizontal scale) has a value of 100, while the next most frequent letter (2) has a value of about 78, and so forth. The Vigenère ciphertext has a remarkably less-telling distribution, although not as pronounced as the completely flat random polyalphabetic cipher. Encyclopædia Britannica, Inc.

The same would be true if digraph or trigraph frequencies were plotted for a sufficiently long ciphertext. In other words, the system is unconditionally secure, not because of any failure on the part of the cryptanalyst to find the right cryptanalytic technique but rather because he is faced with an irresolvable number of choices for the key or plaintext message.

WILLIAM AND ELIZEBETH FRIEDMAN

William F. Friedman and Elizebeth S. Friedman were American cryptologists who helped decipher enemy codes from World War I to World War II.

William Friedman was born on September 24, 1891, in Kishinev, Russia (now Chisinau, Moldova) and was still an infant when his family immigrated to the United States. He studied genetics at Cornell University (B.S., 1914). Elizebeth Smith was born in 1892 in Huntington, Indiana. She

William F. Friedman. National Security Agency/Central Security Service

majored in English at Hillsdale (Michigan) College (B.A., 1915). The two met at the Riverbank Laboratories (Geneva, Illinois), where they both eventually became involved in cryptology, working often for the government in decoding diplomatic messages. They married in May 1917. In 1917–18 William served in the U.S. Army, partly in France, analyzing German code books.

After the war, in 1921, the Friedmans moved to Washington, D.C., where, over the years, Elizebeth Friedman worked for several government departments, notably cracking the codes used by rumrunners and other smugglers, and where William Friedman, in the War Department, became the chief cryptoanalyst in the Signal Intelligence Service, notably leading the teams that broke various Japanese codes, including ultimately the Purple machine cipher initiated by Japan in 1939. After World War II, William Friedman worked awhile for the National Security Agency, and Elizebeth Friedman for the International Monetary Fund. William died on November 2, 1969, in Washington, D.C., and Elizebeth died on October 31, 1980, in Plainfield, New Jersey.

William Friedman wrote *The Index of Coincidence and Its Applications in Cryptography* (1922), one of the standard works in the nomenclature and classification of ciphers. Together, the Friedmans wrote *The Shakespearean Ciphers Examined* (1957), in which they denied Francis Bacon's purported authorship of the William Shakespeare plays and sonnets.

PRODUCT CIPHERS

In the discussion of transposition ciphers it was pointed out that by combining two or more simple transpositions, a more secure encryption may result. In the days of manual cryptography this was a useful device for the cryptographer, and in fact double transposition or product ciphers on key word-based rectangular matrices were widely used. There was also some use of a class of product ciphers known as fractionation systems, wherein a substitution was first made from symbols in the plaintext to multiple symbols (usually pairs, in which case the cipher is called a biliteral cipher) in the ciphertext, which was then encrypted by a final transposition, known as superencryption. One of the most famous field ciphers of all time was a fractionation system, the ADFGVX cipher employed by the German army during World War I. This system used a 6 × 6 matrix to substitution-encrypt the 26 letters and 10 digits into pairs of the symbols A, D, F, G, V, and

X. The resulting biliteral cipher was then written into a rectangular array and route encrypted by reading the columns in the order indicated by a key word, as illustrated in the figure.

bilateral substitution array

	A D F G V X
A	C O 8 X F 4
D	M K 3 A Z 9
F	N W L 0 J D
G	5 S I Y H U
V	P 1 V B 6 R
X	E Q 7 T 2 G

intermediate ciphertext:

W E	A R E	D I S C O V E R E D
FD XA	DG VX XA	FX GF GD AA AD VF XA VX XA FX

S A V E	Y O U R S E L F
GD DG VF XA	GG AD GX VX GD XA FF AV

transposition matrix

A U T H O R
1 6 5 2 3 4
F D X A D G
V X X A F X
G F G D A A
A D V F X A
V X X A F X
G D D G V F
X A G G A D
G X V X G D
X A F F A V

ciphertext:

FVGAV GXGXA ADFAG GXFDF
AXFVA GAGXA AXFDD VXXGV
XDGVF DXFDX DAXA

The ADFGVX cipher, employed by the German army in World War I. Encyclopædia Britannica, Inc.

The great French cryptanalyst Georges J. Painvin succeeded in cryptanalyzing critical ADFGVX ciphers in 1918, with devastating effect for the German army in the battle for Paris.

CHAPTER 3

KEY SYSTEMS AND BLOCK AND STREAM CIPHERS

Cryptographic systems are generically classified (1) by the mathematical operations through which the information (called the "plaintext") is concealed using the encryption key—namely, transposition, substitution, or product ciphers in which two such operations are cascaded; (2) according to whether the transmitter and receiver use the same key (symmetric [single-key] cryptosystem) or different keys (asymmetric [two-key or public-key] cryptosystem); and (3) by whether they produce block or stream ciphers. These three types of system are described in turn here.

SINGLE-KEY CRYPTOGRAPHY

Single-key cryptography is limited in practice by what is known as the key distribution problem. Since all participants must possess the same secret key, if they are physically separated—as is usually the case—there is the problem of how they get the key in the first place. Diplomatic and military organizations traditionally use couriers to distribute keys for the highest-level communications systems, which are then used to superencrypt and distribute keys for lower-level systems. This is impractical, though, for most business and private needs. In addition, key holders are compelled to trust each other unconditionally to protect the keys in their possession and not to misuse them. Again, while this may be a tolerable condition in diplomatic and military organizations, it is almost never acceptable in the commercial realm.

Another key distribution problem is the sheer number of keys required for flexible, secure communications among even a modest number of users. While only a single key is needed for secure communication between two parties, every potential pair of participants in a larger group needs a unique key. To illustrate this point, consider an organization with only 1,000 users: each individual would need a different private key for each of the other 999 users. Such a system would require 499,500 different keys in all, with each user having to protect 999 keys. The number of different keys increases in proportion to the square of the number of users. Secure distribution for so many keys is simply insolvable, as are the demands on the users for the secure storage of their keys. In other words, symmetric key cryptography is impractical in a network in which all participants are equals in all respects. One "solution" is to create a trusted authority—unconditionally trusted by all users—with whom each user can communicate securely to generate and distribute temporary session keys as needed. Each user then has only to protect one key, while the burden for the protection of all of the keys in the network is shifted to the central authority.

TWO-KEY CRYPTOGRAPHY

In 1976, in one of the most inspired insights in the history of cryptology, Sun Microsystems, Inc., computer engineer Whitfield Diffie and Stanford University electrical engineer Martin Hellman realized that the key distribution problem could be almost completely solved if a cryptosystem, T (and perhaps an inverse system, T'), could be devised that used two keys and satisfied the following conditions:

- It must be easy for the cryptographer to calculate a matched pair of keys, e (encryption) and d (decryption), for which $T_e T'_d = I$. Although not essential, it is desirable that $T'_d T_e = I$ and that $T = T'$. Since most of the systems devised to meet points 1–4 satisfy these conditions as well, we will assume they hold hereafter—but that is not necessary.

Whitfield Diffie. Gabriel Bouys/AFP/Getty Images

- The encryption and decryption operation, T, should be (computationally) easy to carry out.
- At least one of the keys must be computationally infeasible for the cryptanalyst to recover even when he knows T, the other key, and arbitrarily many matching plaintext and ciphertext pairs.
- It should not be computationally feasible to recover x given y, where $y = T_k(x)$ for almost all keys k and messages x.

Given such a system, Diffie and Hellman proposed that each user keep his decryption key secret and publish his encryption key in a public directory. Secrecy was not required, either in distributing or in storing this directory of "public" keys. Anyone wishing to communicate privately with a user whose key is in the directory only has to look up the recipient's public key to encrypt a message that only the intended receiver can decrypt. The total number of keys involved is just twice the number of users, with each user having a key in the public directory and his own secret key, which he must protect in his own self-interest. Obviously the public directory must be authenticated, otherwise A could be tricked into communicating with C when he thinks he is communicating with B simply by substituting C's key for B's in A's copy of the directory.

PUBLIC-KEY CRYPTOGRAPHY

Since they were focused on the key distribution problem, Diffie and Hellman called their discovery public-key cryptography. This was the first discussion of two-key cryptography in the open literature. However, Admiral Bobby Inman, while director of the U.S. National Security Agency (NSA) from 1977 to 1981, revealed that two-key cryptography had been known to the agency almost a decade earlier, having been discovered by James Ellis, Clifford Cocks, and Malcolm Williamson at the British Government Code Headquarters (GCHQ).

In this system, ciphers created with a secret key can be decrypted by anyone using the corresponding public key—thereby providing a means to identify the originator at the expense of completely giving up secrecy. Ciphers generated using the public key can only be decrypted by users holding the secret key, not by others holding the public key—however, the secret-key holder receives no information concerning the sender. In other words, the system provides secrecy at the expense of completely giving up any capability of authentication. What Diffie and Hellman had done was to separate the secrecy channel from the authentication channel—a striking example of the sum of the parts being greater than the whole. Single-key cryptography is called symmetric for obvious reasons. A cryptosystem satisfying conditions 1–4 is called asymmetric for equally obvious reasons. There are symmetric cryptosystems in which the encryption and decryption keys are not the same—for example, matrix transforms of the text in which one key is a nonsingular (invertible) matrix and the other its inverse. Even though this is a two-key cryptosystem, since it is easy to calculate the inverse to a non-singular matrix, it does not satisfy condition 3 and is not considered to be asymmetric.

Since in an asymmetric cryptosystem each user has a secrecy channel from every other user to him (using his public key) and an authentication channel from him to all other users (using his secret key), it is possible to achieve both secrecy and authentication using superencryption. Say A wishes to communicate a message in secret to B, but B wants to be sure the message was sent by A. A first encrypts the message with his secret key and then superencrypts the resulting cipher with B's public key. The resulting outer cipher can be decrypted only by B, thus guaranteeing to A that only B can recover the inner cipher. When B opens the inner cipher using A's public key he is certain the message came from someone knowing A's key, presumably A. Simple as it is, this protocol is a paradigm for many contemporary applications.

Cryptographers have constructed several cryptographic schemes of this sort by starting with a "hard" mathematical problem—such as factoring a number that is the product of two very large primes—and attempting to make the cryptanalysis of the scheme be equivalent to solving the hard problem. If this can be done, the cryptosecurity of the scheme will be at least as good as the underlying mathematical problem is hard to solve. This has not been proven for any of the candidate schemes thus far, although it is believed to hold in each instance.

However, a simple and secure proof of identity is possible based on such computational asymmetry. A user first secretly selects two large primes and then openly publishes their product. Although it is easy to compute a modular square root (a number whose square leaves a designated remainder when divided by the product) if the prime factors are known, it is just as hard as factoring (in fact equivalent to factoring) the product if the primes are unknown. A user can therefore prove his identity, i.e., that he knows the original primes, by demonstrating that he can extract modular square roots. The user can be confident that no one can impersonate him since to do so they would have to be able to factor his product. There are some subtleties to the protocol that must be observed, but this illustrates how modern computational cryptography depends on hard problems.

Secret-Sharing

To understand public-key cryptography fully, one must first understand the essentials of one of the basic tools in contemporary cryptology: secret-sharing. There is only one way to design systems whose overall reliability must be greater than that of some critical components—as is the case for aircraft, nuclear weapons, and communications systems—and that is by the appropriate use of redundancy so the system can continue to function even though some components fail. The same is true for information-based systems in which the probability of the security functions being realized must be greater than the probability that some of the participants will not cheat. Secret-sharing, which requires a combination of information held by each participant in order to decipher the key, is a means to enforce concurrence of several participants in the expectation that it is less likely that many will cheat than that one will.

The RSA cryptoalgorithm described in the next section is a two-out-of-two secret-sharing scheme in which each key individually provides no information. Other security functions, such as digital notarization or certification of origination or receipt, depend on more complex sharing of information related to a concealed secret.

RSA ENCRYPTION

The best-known public-key scheme is the Rivest–Shamir–Adleman (RSA) cryptoalgorithm. In this system a user secretly chooses a pair of prime numbers p and q so large that factoring the product $n = pq$ is well beyond projected computing capabilities for the lifetime of the ciphers. At the beginning of the 21st century, U.S. government security standards called for the modulus to be 1,024 bits in size—i.e., p and q each were to be about 155 decimal digits in size, with n roughly a 310-digit number. However, over the following decade, as processor speeds grew and computing techniques became more sophisticated, numbers approaching this size were factored, making it likely that 1,024-bit moduli would soon no longer be safe, and so in 2011 the U.S. government recommended shifting to 2,048-bit moduli.

Having chosen p and q, the user selects an arbitrary integer e less than n and relatively prime to p - 1 and q - 1, that is, so that 1 is the only factor in common between e and the product $(p - 1)(q - 1)$. This assures that there is another number d for which the product ed will leave a remainder of 1 when divided by the least common multiple of p - 1 and q - 1. With knowledge of p and q, the number d can easily be calculated using the Euclidean algorithm. If one does not know p and q, it is equally difficult to find either e or d given the other as to factor n, which is the basis for the cryptosecurity of the RSA algorithm.

We will use the labels d and e to denote the function to which a key is put, but as keys are completely interchangeable, this is only a convenience for exposition. To implement a secrecy channel using the standard two-key version of the RSA cryptosystem, user A would publish e and n in an authenticated public directory but keep d secret. Anyone wishing to send a private message to A would encode it into numbers less than n and then encrypt it using a special formula based on e and n. A can decrypt such a message based on knowing d, but the presumption—and evidence thus far—is that for almost all ciphers no one else can decrypt the message unless he can also factor n.

Similarly, to implement an authentication channel, A would publish d and n and keep e secret. In the simplest use of this channel for identity verification, B can verify that he is in communication with A by looking in the directory to find A's decryption key d and sending him a message to be encrypted. If he gets back a cipher that decrypts to his challenge message using d to decrypt it, he will know that it was in all probability created by someone knowing e and hence that the other communicant is probably A. Digitally signing a message is a more complex operation and requires a cryptosecure "hashing" function. This is a publicly known function that maps any message into a smaller message—called a digest—in which each bit of the digest is dependent on every bit of the message in such a way that changing even one bit in the message is

Prime Numbers

A prime number is any positive integer greater than 1 that is divisible only by itself and 1; e.g., 2, 3, 5, 7, 11, 13, 17, 19, 23, ...

A key result of number theory, called the fundamental theorem of arithmetic, states that every positive integer greater than 1 can be expressed as the product of prime numbers in a unique fashion. Because of this, primes can be regarded as the multiplicative "building blocks" for the natural numbers (all whole numbers greater than zero; e.g., 1, 2, 3, ...).

Primes have been recognized since antiquity, when they were studied by the Greek mathematicians Euclid (fl. c. 300 BCE) and Eratosthenes of Cyrene (c. 276–194 BCE), among others. In his *Elements*, Euclid gave the first known proof that there are infinitely many primes. Various formulas have been suggested for discovering primes, but all have been flawed. Two other famous results concerning the distribution of prime numbers merit special mention: the prime number theorem and the Riemann zeta function.

Since the late 20th century, with the help of computers, prime numbers with millions of digits have been discovered. Like efforts to generate ever more digits of π, such number theory research was thought to have no possible application—that is, until cryptographers discovered how large primes could be used to make nearly unbreakable codes.

apt to change, in a cryptosecure way, half of the bits in the digest. By *cryptosecure* is meant that it is computationally infeasible for anyone to find a message that will produce a preassigned digest and equally hard to find another message with the same digest as a known one. To sign a message—which may not even need to be kept secret— *A* encrypts the digest with the secret *e*, which he appends to the message. Anyone can then decrypt the message using the public key d to recover the digest, which he can also compute independently from the message. If the two agree, he must conclude that A originated the cipher, since only A knew e and hence could have encrypted the message.

Thus far, all proposed two-key cryptosystems exact a very high price for the separation of the privacy or secrecy channel from the authentication or signature channel. The greatly increased amount of computation involved in the asymmetric encryption/decryption process significantly cuts the channel capacity (bits per second of message information communicated). As a result, the main application of two-key cryptography is in hybrid systems. In such a system a two-key algorithm is used for authentication and digital signatures or to exchange a randomly generated session key to be used with a single-key algorithm at high speed for the main communication. At the end of the session this key is discarded.

BLOCK AND STREAM CIPHERS

In general, cipher systems transform fixed-size pieces of plaintext into ciphertext. In older manual systems these pieces were usually single letters or characters—or occasionally, as in the Playfair cipher, digraphs, since this was as large a unit as could feasibly be encrypted and decrypted by hand. Systems that operated on trigrams or larger groups of letters were proposed and understood to be potentially more secure, but they were never implemented because of the difficulty in manual encryption and decryption. In modern single-key cryptography the units of information are often as large as 64 bits, or about $13^{1}/_{2}$ alphabetic characters, whereas two-key cryptography based on the RSA algorithm appears to have settled on 1,024 to 2,048 bits, or between roughly 310 and 620 alphabetic characters, as the unit of encryption.

A block cipher breaks the plaintext into blocks of the same size for encryption using a common key: the block size for a Playfair cipher is two letters, and for the DES used in electronic codebook mode it is 64 bits of binary-encoded plaintext. While a block could consist of a single symbol, normally it is larger.

A stream cipher also breaks the plaintext into units, normally of a single character, and then encrypts the ith unit of the plaintext with the ith unit of a key stream. Vernam encryption with a onetime key is an example of such a system, as are rotor cipher machines and the DES used in the output feedback mode (in which the cipher-text from one encryption is fed back in as the plaintext for the next encryption) to generate a key stream. Stream ciphers depend on the receiver's using precisely the same part of the key stream to decrypt the cipher that was employed to encrypt the plaintext. They thus require that the transmitter's and receiver's key-stream generators be synchronized. This means that they must be synchronized initially and stay in sync thereafter, or else the cipher will be decrypted into a garbled form until synchrony can be reestablished. This latter property of self-synchronizing cipher systems results in what is known as error propagation, an important parameter in any stream-cipher system.

CHAPTER 4

CRYPTANALYSIS

Cryptanalysis, as defined previously, is the art of deciphering or even forging communications that are secured by cryptography. History abounds with examples of the seriousness of the cryptographer's failure and the cryptanalyst's success. In World War II the Battle of Midway, which marked the turning point of the naval war in the Pacific, was won by the United States largely because cryptanalysis had provided Admiral Chester W. Nimitz with information about the Japanese diversionary attack on the Aleutian Islands and about the Japanese order of attack on Midway. Another famous example of cryptanalytic success was the deciphering by the British during World War I of a telegram from the German foreign minister, Arthur Zimmermann, to the German minister in Mexico City, Heinrich von Eckardt, laying out a plan to reward Mexico for entering the war as an ally of Germany. American newspapers published the text (without mentioning the British role in intercepting and decoding the telegram), and the news stories, combined with German submarine attacks on American ships, accelerated a shift in public sentiment for U.S. entry into the war on the side of the Allies. In 1982, during a debate over the Falkland Islands War, a member of Parliament, in a now-famous gaffe, revealed that the British were reading Argentine diplomatic ciphers with as much ease as Argentine code clerks.

Battle of Midway. Keystone/Hulton Archive/Getty Images

BASIC ASPECTS

While cryptography is clearly a science with well-established analytic and synthetic principles, cryptanalysis in the past was as much an art as it was a science. The reason is that success in cryptanalyzing a cipher is as often as not a product of flashes of inspiration, gamelike intuition, and, most important, recognition by the cryptanalyst of pattern or structure, at almost the subliminal level, in the cipher. It is easy to state and demonstrate the principles on which the scientific part of cryptanalysis depends, but it is nearly impossible to convey an appreciation of

THE ZIMMERMANN TELEGRAM

Arthur Zimmermann was born on October 5, 1864, in Marggrabowa, East Prussia (now Olecko, Poland). After a career in the consular service, he won transfer to the diplomatic branch in 1901. Because of the retiring nature of Gottlieb von Jagow, who became foreign secretary in 1913, Zimmermann conducted a large share of the relations with foreign envoys. As acting secretary in Jagow's absence, he participated, with Kaiser Wilhelm II and Chancellor Theobald von Bethmann Hollweg, in Germany's decision of July 5, 1914, to support Austria-Hungary when, after the assassination of Archduke Francis Ferdinand at Sarajevo, Austria-Hungary put pressure on Serbia, thus

The Zimmermann telegram, a coded note that German foreign minister Arthur Zimmermann sent to the German minister in Mexico on January 16, 1917.
© AP Images

angering Russia. Zimmermann drafted the telegram to Vienna embodying Germany's decision, which intensified the crisis that culminated in the outbreak of war.

In 1916, when the German High Command insisted on the resumption of unrestricted submarine warfare as the only remaining weapon to defeat the Allies, even at the risk of provoking the United States into belligerency, Jagow resigned.

On November 25, Zimmermann, who was regarded as "pro-U-boat," was appointed to succeed him. In an effort to nullify or at least to reduce U.S. intervention in Europe by engaging U.S. arms and energies elsewhere, Zimmermann planned to embroil the United States in war with Mexico and Japan. In pursuit of this goal, on January 16, 1917, he sent a secret telegram in code (through the German ambassador in Washington, D.C.) to the German minister in Mexico, authorizing him to propose an alliance to Mexico's President Venustiano Carranza. The offer included "an understanding on our part that Mexico is to reconquer her lost territory in Texas, New Mexico, and Arizona." Carranza was also asked to "invite the immediate adherence of Japan." Intercepted and decoded by British Admiralty intelligence, the telegram was made available to President Woodrow Wilson, who caused it to be published on March 1, 1917. In convincing Americans of German hostility toward the United States, the Zimmermann telegram became one of the factors leading to the U.S. declaration of war against Germany five weeks later.

Zimmermann lost office just after the fall of Bethmann Hollweg's government in the summer of 1917 and never held it again. He died on June 6, 1940, in Berlin.

the art with which the principles are applied. In present-day cryptanalysis, however, mathematics and enormous amounts of computing power are the mainstays.

Cryptanalysis of single-key cryptosystems (described previously) depends on one simple fact—namely, that traces of structure or pattern in the plaintext may survive encryption and be discernible in the ciphertext. Take, for example, the following: in a monoalphabetic substitution cipher (in which each letter is simply replaced by another letter), the frequency with which letters occur in the plaintext alphabet and in the ciphertext alphabet is identical. The cryptanalyst can use this fact in two ways: first, to recognize that he is faced with a monoalphabetic substitution cipher and, second, to aid him in selecting the likeliest equivalences of letters to be tried.

LETTER FREQUENCY DISTRIBUTION FOR A SAMPLE ENGLISH TEXT					
vletter	number of occurrences	frequency	letter	number of occurrences	frequency
E	8,915	0.127	Y	1,891	0.027
T	6,828	0.097	U	1,684	0.024
I	5,260	0.075	M	1,675	0.024
A	5,161	0.073	F	1,488	0.021
O	4,814	0.068	B	1,173	0.017
N	4,774	0.067	G	1,113	0.016
S	4,700	0.067	W	914	0.013
R	4,517	0.064	V	597	0.008
H	3,452	0.049	K	548	0.008
C	3,188	0.045	X	330	0.005
L	2,810	0.04	Q	132	0.002
D	2,161	0.031	Z	65	0.001
P	2,082	0.03	J	56	0.001

The table shows the approximate number of occurrences of each letter in the text of this book, which in turn approximates the raw frequency distribution for most technical material. The following cipher is an encryption of the first sentence of the previous paragraph (minus the parenthetical clause) using a monoalphabetic substitution:

UFMDHQAQTMGRG BX GRAZTW PWM
UFMDHBGMGHWOG VWDWAVG BA BAW
GRODTW XQUH AQOWTM HCQH HFQUWG
BX GHFIUHIFW BF DQHHWFA RA HCW
DTQRAHWLH OQM GIFJRJW WAUFMDHRBA

QAV SW VRGUWFARSTW RA HCW
URDCWFHWLH.

W occurs 21 times in the cipher, H occurs 18, and so on. Even the rankest amateur, using the frequency data in the table, should have no difficulty in recovering the plaintext and all but four symbols of the key in this case.

It is possible to conceal information about raw frequency of occurrence by providing multiple cipher symbols for each plaintext letter in proportion to the relative frequency of occurrence of the letter—i.e., twice as many symbols for E as for S, and so on. The collection of cipher symbols representing a given plaintext letter are called homophones. If the homophones are chosen randomly and with uniform probability when used, the cipher symbols will all occur (on average) equally often in the ciphertext. The great German mathematician Carl Friedrich Gauss (1777–1855) believed that he had devised an unbreakable cipher by introducing homophones. Unfortunately for Gauss and other cryptographers, such is not the case, since there are many other persistent patterns in the plaintext that may partially or wholly survive encryption. Digraphs, for example, show a strong frequency distribution: TH occurring most often, about 20 times as frequently as HT, and so forth. With the use of tables of digraph frequencies that partially survive even homophonic substitution, it is still an easy matter to cryptanalyze a random substitution cipher, though the amount of ciphertext needed grows to a few hundred instead of a few tens of letters.

TYPES OF CRYPTANALYSIS

There are three generic types of cryptanalysis, characterized by what the cryptanalyst knows: (1) ciphertext only, (2) known ciphertext/plaintext pairs, and (3) chosen plaintext or chosen ciphertext. In the discussion of the preceding paragraphs, the cryptanalyst knows only the ciphertext and general structural information about the plaintext. Often the cryptanalyst either will know some of the plaintext or will be able to guess at, and exploit, a likely element of the text, such as a letter beginning with "Dear Sir" or a computer session starting with "LOG IN." The last category represents the most favourable situation for the cryptanalyst, in which he can cause either the transmitter to encrypt a plaintext of his choice or the receiver to decrypt a ciphertext that he chose. Of course, for single-key cryptography there is no distinction between chosen plaintext and chosen ciphertext, but in two-key cryptography it is possible for one of the encryption or decryption functions to be secure against chosen input while the other is vulnerable.

One measure of the security of a cryptosystem is its resistance to standard cryptanalysis; another is its work function, i.e., the amount of computational effort required to search the key space exhaustively. The first can be thought of as an attempt to find an overlooked back door into the system, the other as a brute-force frontal attack. Assume the analyst has only ciphertext available and, with no loss of generality, that it is a block cipher. He could systematically begin decrypting a block of the cipher with one key after another until a block of meaningful text was output (although it would not necessarily be a block of the original plaintext). He would then try that key on the next block of cipher, very much like the technique devised by Friedrich Kasiski to extend a partially recovered key from the probable plaintext attack on a repeated-key Vigenère cipher. If the cryptanalyst has the time and resources to try every key, he will eventually find the right one. Clearly, no cryptosystem can be more secure than its work function.

It is mentioned in the section "Cryptology" in private and commercial life that the 40-bit key cipher systems approved for use in the 1990s were eventually made insecure. There are 2^{40} 40-bit keys possible—very close to 10^{12}—which is the work function of these systems. Most personal computers (PCs) at the end of the 20th century could execute roughly 1,000 MIPS (millions of instructions per second) or 3.6×10^{12} per hour. Testing a key might involve many instructions, but even so a single PC at that time could search a 2^{40}-key space in a matter of hours. Alternatively, partitioning the key space and using multiple machines to carry out the search would have made it possible to produce a solution with PCs of that era in minutes or even seconds. Clearly, by the year 2000, 40-bit keys were not secure by any standard, a situation that brought on the shift to the current 128-bit key.

Because of its reliance on "hard" mathematical problems as a basis for cryptoalgorithms and because one of the keys is publicly exposed, two-key cryptography has led to a new type of cryptanalysis that is virtually indistinguishable from research in any other area of computational mathematics. Unlike the ciphertext attacks or ciphertext/plaintext pair attacks in single-key cryptosystems, this sort of cryptanalysis is aimed at breaking the cryptosystem by analysis that can be carried out based only on a knowledge of the system itself. Obviously there is no counterpart to this kind of cryptanalytic attack in single-key systems.

Similarly, the RSA cryptoalgorithm (described in the section "RSA Encryption") is susceptible to a breakthrough in factoring techniques. In 1970 the world record in factoring was 39 digits. In 2009 the record was a 768-digit RSA challenge. That achievement explains why standards in 2011 called for moving beyond the standard 1,024-bit key (310 digits) to a 2,048-bit key (620 digits) in order to be confident of security through approximately 2030. In other words, the security of two-key cryptography depends on well-defined mathematical questions in a way that single-key cryptography generally does not; conversely, it equates cryptanalysis with mathematical research in an atypical way.

EARLY MANUAL AND MECHANICAL CRYPTOGRAPHY

The first well-defined phase in the history of cryptology was the period of manual cryptography, starting with the origins of the subject in antiquity and continuing through World War I. Throughout this phase cryptography was limited by the complexity of what a code clerk could reasonably do aided by simple mnemonic devices. As a result, ciphers were limited to at most a few pages in size, i.e., to only a few thousands of characters. General principles for both cryptography and cryptanalysis were known, but the security that could be achieved was always limited by what could be done manually. Most systems could be cryptanalyzed, therefore, given sufficient ciphertext and effort. One way to think of this phase is that any cryptography scheme devised during those two millennia could have equally well been used by the ancients if they had known of it.

A second phase came with the mechanization of cryptography, which began shortly after World War I and continues even today. The applicable technology involved either telephone and telegraph communications (employing punched paper tape, telephone switches, and relays) or calculating machines such as the Brunsvigas, Marchants, Facits, and Friedens (employing gears, sprockets, ratchets, pawls, and cams). This resulted in the rotor machines used by all participants in World War II. These machines could realize far more complex operations than were feasible manually and, more importantly, they could encrypt and decrypt faster and with less chance of error.

THE FIRST SYSTEMS

People have probably tried to conceal information in written form from the time that writing developed. Examples survive in stone inscriptions, cuneiform tablets, and papyruses showing that the ancient Egyptians, Hebrews, Babylonians, and Assyrians all devised protocryptographic systems both to deny information to the uninitiated and to enhance its significance when it was revealed. The first recorded use of cryptography for correspondence was by the Spartans, who as early as 400 BCE employed a cipher device called the scytale for secret communication between military commanders. The scytale consisted of a tapered baton, around which was spirally wrapped a strip of parchment or leather on which the message was then written. When unwrapped, the letters were scrambled in order and formed the cipher; however, when the strip was wrapped around another baton of identical proportions to the original, the plaintext reappeared. Thus, the Greeks were the inventors of the first transposition cipher. During the 4th century BCE, Aeneas Tacticus wrote a work entitled *On the Defense of Fortifications*, one chapter of which was devoted to cryptography, making it the earliest treatise on the subject. Another Greek, Polybius (*c.* 200–118 BCE), devised a means of encoding letters into pairs of symbols by a device called the Polybius checkerboard, which is a true biliteral substitution and presages many elements of later cryptographic systems. Similar examples of primitive substitution or transposition ciphers abound in the history of other civilizations. The Romans used monoalphabetic substitution with a simple cyclic displacement of the alphabet. Julius Caesar employed a shift of three positions so that plaintext A was encrypted as D, while Augustus Caesar used a shift of one position so that plaintext A was enciphered as B. As many moviegoers noticed, HAL, the computer in *2001: A Space Odyssey* (1968), encrypts to IBM using Augustus's cipher.

The first people to understand clearly the principles of cryptography and to elucidate the beginnings of cryptanalysis were the Arabs. They devised and used both substitution and transposition ciphers and discovered the use of both letter frequency distributions and probable plaintext in cryptanalysis. As a result, by about 1412, al-Kalka-shandī could include a respectable, if elementary, treatment of several cryptographic systems in his encyclopaedia *Ṣubīal-aīshī* and give explicit instructions on how to cryptanalyze ciphertext using letter frequency counts complete with lengthy examples to illustrate the technique.

European cryptology dates from the Middle Ages, when it was developed by the Papal States and the Italian city-states. The first European manual on cryptography (*c.* 1379) was a compilation of ciphers by Gabriele de Lavinde of Parma, who served Pope Clement VII. This manual, now in the Vatican archives, contains a set of keys for 24 correspondents and embraces symbols for letters, nulls, and several two-character code equivalents for words and names. The first brief code vocabularies, called nomenclators, were gradually expanded and became the mainstay well into the 20th century for diplomatic communications of nearly all European governments. In 1470 Leon Battista Alberti published *Trattati in cifra* ("Treatise on Ciphers"), in which he described the first cipher disk; he prescribed that the setting of the disk should be changed

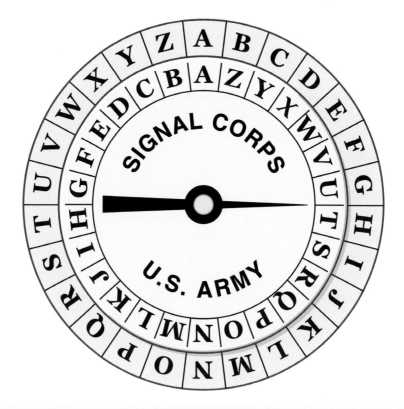

Used in the field by the U.S. Army Signal Corps at the beginning of World War I, the disk enabled messages to be quickly encrypted with a simple substitution cipher by rotating the inner ring. Encyclopædia Britannica, Inc.

after enciphering three or four words, thus conceiving of the notion of polyalphabeticity. This same device was used almost five centuries later by the U.S. Army Signal Corps for tactical communications in World War I. Giambattista della Porta provided a modified form of a square encryption/decryption table and the earliest example of a digraphic cipher in *De furtivis literarum notis* (1563; "The Notorious Secret Literature"). The *Traicté des chiffres* ("Treatise on Ciphers"), published in 1586 by Blaise de Vigenère, contains the square encryption/decryption table bearing his name and descriptions of the first plaintext and ciphertext autokey systems.

By the time of the American Civil War, diplomatic communications were generally secured using codes, and cipher systems had become a rarity for this application because of their perceived weakness and inefficiency. Cipher systems prevailed, however, for military tactical communications because of the difficulty of protecting codebooks from capture or compromise in the field. In the early history of the United States, codes were widely used, as were book ciphers. Book ciphers approximate onetime keys if the book used is lost or unknown. (A famous unsolved book cipher is the Beale cipher [*c.* 1820], which purports to give the location of a buried treasure in Bedford county, Virginia.) During the Civil War the Union Army made extensive use of transposition ciphers, in which a key word indicated the order in which columns of the array were to be read and in which the elements were either plaintext words or code word replacements for plaintext. The Confederate Army primarily used the Vigenère cipher and on occasion simple monoalphabetic substitution. While Union cryptanalysts solved most intercepted Confederate ciphers, the Confederacy in desperation sometimes published Union ciphers in newspapers, appealing for help from readers in cryptanalyzing them.

WORLD WARS I AND II

During the first two years of World War I, code systems were used for high-command and diplomatic communications, just as they had been for centuries, and cipher systems were used almost exclusively for tactical communications. Field cipher systems such as the U.S. Signal Corps's cipher disk mentioned previously, lacked sophistication (and security), however. Nevertheless, by the end of the war some complicated cipher systems were used for high-level communications, the most famous of which was the German ADFGVX fractionation cipher, described in the section "Product Ciphers."

The communications needs of telegraphy and radio and the maturing of mechanical and electromechanical technology came together in the 1920s to bring about a major advance in cryptodevices: the development of rotor cipher machines. Although the concept of a rotor had been anticipated in the older mechanical cipher disks, American Edward H. Hebern recognized in about 1917 (and made the first patent claim) that by hardwiring a monoalphabetic substitution in the connections from contacts on one side of an electrical disk (rotor) to contacts on the other side and then cascading a collection of such rotors, polyalphabetic substitutions of almost arbitrary complexity could be realized. A set of these rotors is usually arranged in a stack called a basket; the rotation of each of the rotors in the stack causes the next one to rotate, much as the wheels in an odometer advance $1/_{10}$ of a revolution for every full revolution of its driving wheel. In operation, the rotors in the stack provide an electrical path from contact to contact through all of the rotors. In a straight-through rotor system, closing the key contact on a typewriter-like keyboard sends a current to one of the contacts on the end rotor. The current then passes through the maze of interconnections defined by the remaining rotors in the stack and their relative rotational positions to a point on the output end plate, where it is connected to either a printer or an indicator, thereby outputting the ciphertext letter equivalent to the input plaintext letter.

Until 2003, Hebern was generally recognized as the inventor of the rotor encryption machine. In that year, scholars published research showing that in 1915, two years before Hebern's work, a rotor machine had been designed and built by two Dutch naval officers, Lieutenant R.P.C. Spengler and Lieutenant Theo van Hengel, a second prototype built by a Dutch mechanical engineer and wireless operator, Lieutenant W.K. Maurits, and the devices tested by the Dutch navy in the East Indies under the direction of Rear Admiral F. Bauduin. The navy declined to proceed with the project, however, and the participants did not immediately pursue a patent. At the end of World War I, Spengler and van Hengel sought to patent their idea, but the navy resisted declassifying their work. Meanwhile, Hebern had filed a patent claim in 1917, which held up through the years, and gradually the Dutch inventors were forgotten.

Starting in 1921 and continuing through the next decade, Hebern constructed a series of steadily improving rotor machines that were evaluated by the U.S. Navy and undoubtedly led to the United States' superior position in cryptology as compared to that of the Axis powers during World War II. The 1920s were marked by a series of challenges by inventors of cipher machines to national cryptologic services and by one service to another, resulting in a steady improvement of both cryptomachines and techniques for the analysis of machine ciphers. At almost the same time that Hebern was developing the rotor cipher machine in the United States, European engineers, notably Hugo A. Koch of the Netherlands and Arthur Scherbius of Germany, independently discovered the rotor concept and designed machines that became the precursors of the best-known cipher machine in history, the German Enigma used in World War II.

Another type of rotor machine is much more like the Vernam encryption system (described previously in "Substitution Ciphers"). Such devices are pin-and-lug machines, and they typically consist of a collection of rotors having a prime number of labeled positions on each rotor. At each position a small pin can be set to an active or inactive position. In operation, all of the rotors advance one position at each step. Therefore, if the active pin settings are chosen appropriately, the machine will not recycle to its initial pin configuration until it has been advanced a number of steps equal to the product of the number of positions in each one of the rotors. One machine of this type, the Hagelin M-209 (named for the Swedish engineer Boris Hagelin), was used extensively by the U.S. military for tactical field communications during World War II. In the M-209 the rotors have 26, 25, 23, 21, 19, and 17 positions, respectively, so that the key

The German navy employed various versions of the Enigma cipher machine during the war, including this four-rotor model.

Hagelin design M-209 U.S. cipher machine used for tactical communications during World War II.

Although no Japanese Purple cipher machines survived the war, this is a functional analog of the Japanese machine that was operational from 1939.

The Japanese Jade cipher machine was a variant of the Purple cipher machines in use during the war. It differed primarily in that Japanese kana characters could be typed directly on the keyboard.

period length is 101,405,850. (It is interesting to note that this length key would be exhausted in $\frac{1}{100}$ of a second on an Internet backbone circuit today.)

The relationship of this machine to the Vernam encryption system is not only through the way in which a lengthy binary sequence of active pin settings in the rotors is achieved by forming the product of six much shorter ones, but also in the way a symbol of plaintext is encrypted using the resulting key stream. Just behind the rotors is a "squirrel cage" consisting of 27 bars on each of which is a pair of movable lugs. Either or both of the lugs can be set in a position to be engaged and moved to the left on each step by a diverter actuated by the presence of an active pin on the corresponding rotor. The result is an effective gear wheel in which the number of teeth is determined by both the active pin settings and the movable lug settings. The number of teeth set determines the cyclical shift between one direct alphabet (plaintext) ABC...

ALAN TURING'S BOMBE

The Enigma machine, looking rather like a typewriter, was battery-powered and highly portable. In addition to a keyboard, the device had a lamp board consisting of 26 stenciled letters, each with a small lightbulb behind it. Each bulb in the lamp board was electrically connected to a letter on the keyboard, but the wiring passed via a number of rotating wheels, with the result that the connections were always changing as the wheels moved. Thus, typing the same letter at the keyboard, such as AAAA..., would produce a stream of changing letters at the lamp board, such as WMEV.... It was this ever-changing pattern of connections that made Enigma extremely hard to break.

In the winter of 1932–33, Polish mathematician Marian Rejewski deduced the pattern of wiring inside the three rotating wheels of the Enigma machine. (Rejewski was helped by photographs, received from the French secret service, showing pages of an Enigma operating manual.) Before an Enigma operator began enciphering a message, he set Enigma's three wheels (four in models used by the German navy) to various starting positions that were also known to the intended recipient. In a major breakthrough, Rejewski invented a method for finding out, from each intercepted German transmission, the positions in which the wheels had started at the beginning of the message. In consequence, Poland was able to read encrypted German messages from 1933 to 1939.

In the summer of 1939 Poland turned over everything— including information about Rejewski's Bomba, a machine he devised in 1938 for breaking Enigma messages—to Britain and France. New methods developed during 1940 at Bletchley Park, a British government establishment located north of London, enabled code breakers there to continue to decipher German air force and army communications, and in June 1941 British mathematician Alan M. Turing and his group succeeded in breaking into the daily communications of the German navy's U-boats. Great care was always exercised to conceal the fact that Bletchley had deciphered these messages. For instance, British intelligence leaked false information hinting at revolutionary new developments in long-range radar.

In March 1940, Turing's first Bombe, a code-breaking machine, was installed at Bletchley Park; improvements suggested by British mathematician Gordon Welchman were incorporated by August. This complex machine consisted of approximately 100 rotating drums, 10 miles of wire, and about 1 million soldered connections. The Bombe searched through different possible positions of Enigma's internal wheels, looking for a pattern of keyboard-to-lamp board connections that would turn coded letters into plain German. The method depended on human instinct, though; to initiate the process, a code breaker had to guess a few words in the message (these guessed words were called a crib). The Polish Bomba, a simpler 18-drum machine, was a forerunner of the Bombe, but it was based on Rejewski's method for finding the wheel positions at the start of the message. Unlike Rejewski's method, the more powerful crib-based method invented by Turing survived the May 1940 change. The war on Enigma was transformed by the high-speed Bombes, and more of them were installed in Britain and the United States.

and a reverse standard alphabet ZYX....Thus, if no tooth were present, A would encrypt to Z, B to Y, and so forth, while one tooth present would cause A to encrypt to Y, B to Z, etc. This is strictly a Vernam-type encryption—i.e., encryption by subtraction modulo 26 of the key symbol from the plaintext symbol. To decrypt, the ciphertext is processed with the same pin settings that were used to encrypt it but with the cyclical shift set to occur in the opposite direction.

In 1930 the Japanese Foreign Office put into service its first rotor machine, which was code-named Red by U.S. cryptanalysts. In 1935–36 the U.S. Army Signal Intelligence Service (SIS) team of cryptanalysts, led by William F. Friedman, succeeded in cryptanalyzing Red ciphers, drawing heavily on its previous experience in cryptanalyzing the machine ciphers produced by the Hebern rotor machines. In 1939 the Japanese introduced a new cipher machine, code-named Purple by U.S. cryptanalysts, in which rotors were replaced by telephone stepping switches. Because the replacement of Red machines by Purple machines was gradual, providing an enormous number of cribs between the systems to aid cryptanalysts, and because the Japanese had taken a shortcut to avoid the key distribution problem by generating keys systematically, U.S. cryptanalysts were able not only to cryptanalyze the Purple ciphers but also eventually to anticipate keys several days in advance. Functionally equivalent analogs to the Purple cipher machines were constructed by Friedman and his SIS associates and used throughout the war to decrypt Japanese ciphers. Apparently no Purple machine survived the war. Another Japanese cipher machine, code-named Jade, was essentially the same as the Purple. It differed from the latter chiefly in that it typed Japanese kana characters directly.

The greatest triumphs in the history of cryptanalysis were the Polish and British solution of the German Enigma ciphers and of two teleprinter ciphers, whose output was code-named Ultra, and the American cryptanalysis of the Japanese Red, Orange, and Purple ciphers, code-named Magic. These developments played a major role in the Allies' conduct of World War II. Of the two, the cryptanalysis of the Japanese ciphers is the more impressive, because it was a tour de force of cryptanalysis against ciphertext alone. In the case of the Enigma machines, the basic patents had been issued in the United States, commercial machines were widely available, and the rotor designs were known to Allied cryptanalysts from a German code clerk. Although such factors do not diminish the importance of the Ultra intercepts, they did make the cryptanalysis easier.

CHAPTER 6

MODERN ELECTRONIC CRYPTOGRAPHY

With the invention of electromechanical rotor machines after World War I, the secure size of ciphers grew accordingly, so that tens or even hundreds of thousands of characters were feasible. After World War II, a switch from electromechanical devices to electronic ones accelerated this trend. To illustrate the progress that was made in only eight decades, in 1999 the U.S. government designed and fabricated a single silicon chip implementation of the Data Encryption Standard (DES) with a demonstrated throughput of 6.7 billion bits (6.7 gigabits) per second. The Advanced Encryption Standard (AES), meanwhile, could be implemented in a single silicon chip to handle 10^{10} bits per second (10 gigabits per second) on an Internet backbone circuit. In a few seconds of operation, trillions of bits of cipher could be processed, compared with the tens of bits per second possible with the first mechanized cipher machines. By the beginning of the 21st century the volume of ciphertext that had to be dealt with on a single communications channel had increased nearly a billionfold, and it continues to increase at an ever-expanding rate.

The last two decades of the 20th century marked the most radical change of all in the history of cryptology—its dramatic extension to the information age: digital signatures, authentication, shared or distributed capabilities to exercise cryptologic functions, and so on. It is tempting to equate this phase with the appearance of public-key cryptography, but that is too narrow a view. Cryptology's third phase was the inevitable consequence of having to devise ways for electronic information to perform all of the functions that had historically been done with the aid of tangible documents.

THE IMPACT OF ELECTRONICS

In the years immediately following World War II, the electronic technology developed in support of radar and the recently discovered digital computer was adapted to cryptomachines. The first such devices were little more than rotor machines in which rotors had been replaced by electronically realized substitutions. The advantage of these electronic machines was speed of operation; the disadvantages were the cryptanalytic weaknesses inherited from mechanical rotor machines and the principle of cyclically shifting simple substitutions for realizing more complex product substitutions. In fact, rotor machines and electronic machines coexisted into the 1970s and early '80s. There is little information in the open literature about the electronic cipher machines used by the various national cryptologic services, so the most reliable indication of cryptographic developments in the period from the final generation of rotor machines — the KL-7 developed by the United States for the North Atlantic Treaty Organization (NATO) — to the appearance of DES and public-key systems in 1976 is to be found in commercial equipment. (The KL-7 was withdrawn from service in June 1983; in 1985 it was learned that the Walker family spy ring had turned over a KL-7 device and keying material to the Soviets.)

One class of electronic devices that function similar to rotors is the Fibonacci generator (also called the Koken generator after its inventor), named for the Fibonacci sequence of number theory. In the classical Fibonacci sequence 1, 1, 2, 3, 5, 8, 13...each successive term, beginning with 2, is the sum of the two terms to its left; i.e., $F_i = F_{i-1} + F_{i-2}$. By loose analogy, any sequence in which each term is the sum of a collection of earlier terms in fixed (relative) locations is called a Fibonacci sequence.

In an n-stage Fibonacci generator the contents of an n-bit shift register are shifted right one position at each step—the bit at the extreme right being shifted out and lost—and the new left-hand bit is determined by the logical sum ($1 + 1 = 1$, $0 + 1 = 1 + 0 = 0 + 0 = 0$; symbolized by $\oplus$) of bits occurring in prescribed locations in the shift register before the shift was made. For example, for n = 5 and $x_i = x_{i-1} \oplus x_{i-4} \oplus x_{i-5}$ one obtains the 31-bit cycle 0101110110001111100110100100001, which is the maximal-length sequence realizable with a five-stage generator. The relevance of Fibonacci generators to cryptography is seen if the sequence is read five bits at a time by successively shifting one bit position to the left. This yields a scrambled ordering of the integers 1 through 31 that resembles the scrambled ordering produced by rotors.

The cryptographic problem is that the combining operation used to determine successive states in the sequence is linear and hence easily invertible, even though the sequence can be $2^n - 1$ bits in length before repeating. Another problem is how the key is to be used. The obvious choice—i.e., simply to use the key to determine the number of steps in the cycle from the plaintext n-tuple to the ciphertext n-tuple—is cryptographically insecure because a known plaintext cryptanalysis would quickly reveal the key. A frequently reinvented solution to this problem has been to use the number found in selected locations of one maximal-length feedback shift register, in which the key is used as the initial register fill, to control the number of steps from the plaintext n-tuple to the ciphertext n-tuple in the cycle of another linear feedback shift register. In schemes of this sort the key register is generally stepped forward to hide the key itself before any encryption of plaintext is carried out and then advanced sufficiently many steps between encryptions to ensure diffusion of the keying variables. To encrypt an n-bit block of plaintext, the text is loaded into the main shift register and the machine stepped through a specified number of steps, normally a multiple of the number of bits in the key, sufficient to diffuse the information in the plaintext and in the key over all positions in the resulting ciphertext. To decrypt the resulting ciphertext it is necessary to have an inverse combiner function or for the original encryption function to be involutory—i.e., the encryption and decryption functions are identical, so that encrypting the ciphertext restores the plaintext. It is not difficult to design the feedback logic to make an involutory machine. Pictorially, the machine has simply retraced its steps in the cycle(s). Linearity in the logic, though, is a powerful aid to the cryptanalyst, especially if a matched plaintext/ciphertext attack is possible.

With a slight modification, this approach constitutes the basis of several commercially available cryptographic devices that function in a manner quite similar to the pin-and-lug cipher machines previously described. One such cryptomachine has six maximal-length linear feedback shift registers in which the stepping is controlled by another shift register; the contents of the latter are used to address a (nonlinear) lookup table defined by keys supplied by the user.

FIBONACCI'S NUMBERS

Leonardo Fibonacci was a medieval mathematician from the northern Italian city of Pisa. Known to history either as Leonardo Pisano or simply as Fibonacci, he gained fame throughout Europe for his *Liber abaci* ("Book of the Abacus"), which he published in 1202 and which was the first European work on Hindu-Arabic numerals. He is known to modern mathematicians mainly because of the Fibonacci sequence, derived from a problem in the *Liber abaci:*

> *A certain man put a pair of rabbits in a place surrounded on all sides by a wall. How many pairs of rabbits can be produced from that pair in a year if it is supposed that every month each pair begets a new pair which from the second month on becomes productive?*

The resulting number sequence, 1, 1, 2, 3, 5, 8, 13, 21, 34, 55 (Leonardo himself omitted the first term), in which each number is the sum of the two preceding numbers, is the first recursive number sequence (in which the relation between two or more successive terms can be expressed by a formula) known in Europe. Terms in the sequence were stated in a formula by the French-born mathematician Albert Girard in 1634: $u_{n+2} = u_{n+1} + u_n$, in which u represents the term and the subscript its rank in the sequence. The mathematician Robert Simson at the University of Glasgow in 1753 noted that, as the numbers increased in magnitude, the ratio between succeeding numbers approached the number a, the golden ratio, whose value is 1.6180 . . . , or $(1 + 5)/2$.

In the 19th century the term Fibonacci sequence was coined by the French mathematician Edouard Lucas, and scientists began to discover such sequences in nature; for example, in the spirals of sunflower heads, in pine cones, in the regular descent (genealogy) of the male bee, in the related logarithmic (equiangular) spiral in snail shells, in the arrangement of leaf buds on a stem, and in animal horns.

To avoid the problems associated with linearity, cryptographers have devised a number of nonlinear feedback logics that possess such desirable properties as diffusion of information (to spread the effects of small changes in the text) and large-cycle structure (to prevent exhaustive search) but which are computationally infeasible to invert working backward from the output sequence to the initial state(s), even with very many pairs of matched plaintext/ciphertext. The nonlinear feedback logic, used to determine the next bit in the sequence, can be employed in much the same way as linear feedback logic. The complicating effect of the key on the ciphertext in nonlinear logic, however, greatly contributes to the difficulty faced by the cryptanalyst. Electronic cipher machines of this general type were widely used, both commercially and by national cryptologic services.

The significance of the above historical remarks is that they lead in a natural way to the most widely adopted and used cipher in the history of cryptography—the Data Encryption Standard (DES).

DES AND AES

In 1973 the U.S. National Bureau of Standards (NBS; now the National Institute of Standards and Technology) issued a public request for proposals for a cryptoalgorithm to be considered for a new cryptographic standard. No viable submissions were received. A second request was issued in 1974, and International Business Machines (IBM) submitted the patented Lucifer algorithm that had been devised by one of the company's researchers, Horst Feistel, a few years earlier. The Lucifer algorithm was evaluated in secret consultations between the NBS and the National Security Agency (NSA). After some modifications to the internal functions and a shortening of the key size from 112 bits to 56 bits, the full details of the algorithm that was to become the Data Encryption Standard (DES) were published in the *Federal Register* in 1975. Following almost two years of public evaluation and comment, the standard itself was adopted at the end of 1976 and published at the beginning of 1977. As a consequence of certification of the standard by the NBS and its commitment to evaluate and certify implementations, it was mandated that the DES be used in unclassified U.S. government applications for the protection of binary-coded data during transmission and storage in computer systems and networks and on a case-by-case basis for the protection of classified information.

The use of the DES algorithm was made mandatory for all financial transactions of the U.S. government involving electronic fund transfer, including those conducted by member banks of the Federal Reserve System. Subsequent adoption of the DES by standards organizations worldwide caused the DES to become a de facto international standard for business and commercial data security as well.

The DES is a product block cipher in which 16 iterations, or rounds, of substitution and transposition (permutation) process are cascaded. The block size is 64 bits. The key, which controls the transformation, also consists of 64 bits; however, only 56 of these can be chosen by the user and are actually key bits. The remaining eight are parity check bits and hence totally redundant. The figure is a functional schematic of the sequence of events that occurs in one round of the DES encryption (or decryption) transformation. At each intermediate stage of the transformation process, the cipher output from the preceding stage is partitioned into the 32 left-most bits, L_i, and the 32 right-most bits, R_i. R_i is transposed to become the left-hand part of the next higher intermediate cipher,

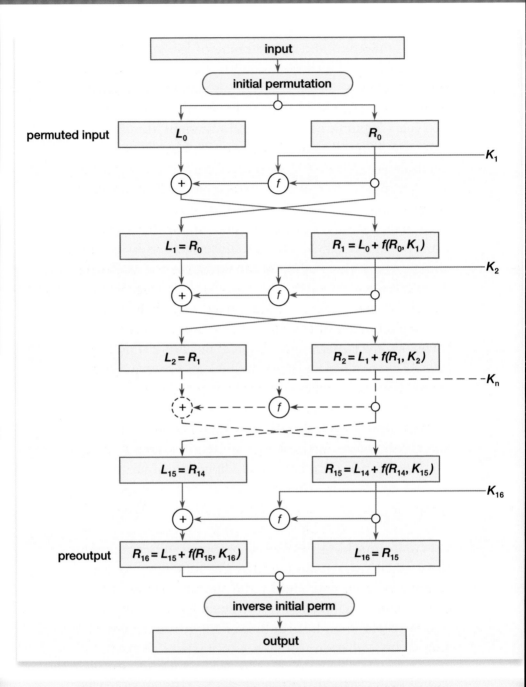

Flow diagram for the 16-step Data Encryption Standard (DES) operation. From Data Encryption Standard, FIPS Publ. no. 46, National Bureau of Standards, 1977

L_{i+1}. The right-hand half of the next cipher, R_{i+1}, however, is a complex function, $L_i + f(R_i, K_{i+1})$, of a subset of the key bits, K_{i+1}, and of the entire preceding intermediate cipher. The essential feature to the security of the DES is that f involves a very special nonlinear substitution—i.e., $f(A) + f(B) \neq f(A + B)$—specified by the Bureau of Standards in tabulated functions known as S boxes. This process is repeated 16 times. This basic structure, in which at each iteration the cipher output from the preceding step is divided in half and the halves transposed with a complex function controlled by the key being performed on the right half and the result combined with the left half using the "exclusive-or" from logic (true or "1" only when exactly one of the cases is true) to form the new right half, is called a Feistel cipher and is widely used—and not just in the DES. One of the attractive things about Feistel ciphers— in addition to their security—is that if the key subsets are used in reverse order, repeating the "encryption" decrypts a ciphertext to recover the plaintext.

The security of the DES is no greater than its work factor—the brute-force effort required to search 2^{56} keys. That is a search for a needle in a haystack of 72 quadrillion straws. In 1977 that was considered an impossible computational task. In 1999 a special-purpose DES search engine combined with 100,000 personal computers on the Internet to find a DES challenge key in 22 hours. An earlier challenge key was found by the distributed Internet computers in 39 days and by the special-purpose search engine alone in 3 days. For some time it has been apparent that the DES, though never broken in the usual cryptanalytic sense, was no longer secure. A way was devised that effectively gave the DES a 112-bit key—ironically, the key size of the Lucifer algorithm originally proposed by IBM in 1974. This is known as "triple DES" and involves using two normal DES keys. As proposed by Walter Tuchman of the Amperif Corporation, the encryption operation would be $E_I D_2 E_I$ while decryption would be $D_I E_2 D_I$. Since $E_k D_k = D_k E_k = I$ for all keys k, this triple encryption uses an inverse pair of operations. There are many ways to choose the three operations so that the resultant will be such a pair; Tuchman suggested this scheme since if the two keys are both the same, it becomes an ordinary single-key DES. Thus, equipment with triple DES could be interoperable with equipment that only implemented the older single DES. Banking standards have adopted this scheme for security.

It may seem that DES is very different from the cryptosystems that preceded it—except that it is a product cipher made up of transpositions and substitutions— but it is in fact a logical continuation of them. In a sense the DES was the logical culmination of a long history of development of single-key cryptographic algorithms, and it is this aspect that has been emphasized in the discussion thus far. In another sense, however, the DES is quite different from anything that preceded it. Cryptology has traditionally been a secretive science, so much so that it was only at the end of the 20th century that the principles on which the cryptanalysis of the Japanese and German cipher machines of World War II were based were declassified and released. What is different about the DES is that it is a totally public cryptographic algorithm. Every detail of its operations—enough to permit anyone who wishes to program it on a microcomputer—is widely available in published form and on the Internet. The paradoxical result is that what is generally conceded to have been one of the best cryptographic systems in the history of cryptology was also the least secret.

In January 1997 the National Institute of Standards and Technology (NIST) issued a public request to submit candidates to replace the aging DES. This time 15 viable submissions from 12 countries were received. In October 2000 NIST announced that Rijndael, a program created by two Belgian cryptographers, Joan Daemen and Vincent Rijmen, had been accepted as the new standard, or the Advanced Encryption Standard (AES). The NBS had expected the DES to be implemented in special-purpose hardware and hence had given little or no consideration to its efficient implementation in software, i.e., using general-purpose microprocessors. As a result, the DES was unable to take advantage of the rapid development in microprocessors that occurred in the last two decades of the 20th century. The AES specifications, on the other hand, emphasized hardware and software implementations equally. In part, this recognized the needs of smart cards and other point-of-sale equipment, which typically have very limited computational capabilities, but more important was a recognition of the growing needs of the Internet and e-commerce. Based on their experience with the DES, where improvements in computing simply overran the work factor of the fixed 56-bit key, NIST specifications for the AES also called for the algorithm to be capable of increasing the key length if necessary. Rijndael proved itself to be both small enough to be implemented on smart cards (at less than 10,000 bytes of code) and flexible enough to allow longer key lengths.

Based on the DES experience, there is every reason to believe the AES will not succumb to cryptanalysis, nor will it be overrun by developments in computing, as was the DES, since its work factor can easily be adjusted to outpace them.

CONCLUSION

In the computer age, data security is an issue that has moved far beyond the narrow circles of military defense and diplomacy to include the innumerable transactions of everyday life. Data residing on a computer anywhere is under threat of being stolen, destroyed, or modified maliciously. This is true whenever the computer is accessible to multiple users but is particularly significant when the computer is accessible over a network such as the Internet. The first line of defense is to allow access to a computer only to authorized, trusted users and to authenticate those users by a password or similar mechanism. But clever programmers have learned how to evade such mechanisms. The need to protect sensitive data (for personal as well as national security) has led to extensive research in cryptography and the development of encryption standards for providing a high level of confidence that the data are safe from decoding by even the most powerful computer attacks. Computer theft, however, is not just the theft of information from a computer; it is also theft by use of a computer, typically by modifying data. If a bank's records are not adequately secure, for example, someone could set up a false account and transfer money into it from valid accounts for later withdrawal. Such violations of security harm the entire public, and at the same time advances in cryptographic systems benefit the entire public—including the vast majority of people who never suspect that these systems underlie the keystrokes and mouse clicks that complete their purchases, pay their bills, and send their messages.

GLOSSARY

algorithm A step-by-step procedure for solving a problem or accomplishing some end, especially by a computer.

alphanumeric Consisting of both letters and numbers and often other symbols (as punctuation marks and mathematical symbols).

ASCII A code for representing alphanumeric information.

autokey A cipher that encrypts a plaintext message.

biliteral Consisting of two letters.

cipher A combination of symbolic letters.

cryptanalysis The art of deciphering or even forging communications that are secured by cryptography.

cryptography Practice of the enciphering and deciphering of messages in secret code in order to render them unintelligible to all but the intended receiver.

cryptology The scientific study of cryptography and cryptanalysis.

cryptosecurity The practice of developing secure cryptosystems and implementing them effectively.

cryptosystem A system of algorithms designed to enable some form of encryption or decryption.

decrypt To decode.

encrypt To disguise information as "ciphertext," or data unintelligible to an unauthorized person.

lexicography The principles and practices of dictionary making.

matrix A rectangular array of mathematical elements (as the coefficients of simultaneous linear equations) that can be combined to form sums and products with similar arrays having an appropriate number of rows and columns.

microprocessor Any of a type of miniature electronic device that contains the control circuitry necessary to perform the functions of a digital computer's central processing unit.

mnemonic A formula or rhyme intended to assist the memory.

monoalphabetic The decryption system that uses the same fixed mappings from plaintext to cipher letters.

plaintext The intelligible form of an encrypted text or of its elements.

polyalphabetic The decryption system that uses the multiple mappings from plaintext to cipher letters.

recursive Of, relating to, or constituting a procedure that can repeat itself indefinitely.

rotor machine A device used for encrypting and decrypting secret messages.

scytale A cylindrical instrument designed to perform a transposition cipher.

theorem A formula, proposition, or statement in mathematics or logic deduced or to be deduced from other formulas or propositions.

BIBLIOGRAPHY

David Kahn, *The Codebreakers: The Story of Secret Writing*, rev. ed. (1996), is a comprehensive and meticulously researched history of classical single-key cryptology. Simon Singh, *The Code Book: The Science of Secrecy from Ancient Egypt to Quantum Cryptography* (2000), the North American edition of a book by a British science writer and television producer, describes the importance of code-making and codebreaking through history.

Fred Piper and Sean Murphy, *Cryptography: A Very Short Introduction* (2002), is written for the general reader. Modern texts in cryptography include Christof Paar and Jan Pelzl, *Understanding Cryptography: A Textbook for Students and Practitioners* (2010); Bruce Schneier, *Applied Cryptography: Protocols, Algorithms, and Source Code in C*, 2nd ed. (1996); and Alfred J. Menezes, Paul C. van Oorschot, and Scott A. Vanstone, *Handbook of Applied Cryptography* (1997), all providing very complete coverage of cryptological protocols and algorithms.

Two books on the Ultra intelligence project of World War II are David Kahn, *Seizing the Enigma: The Race to Break the German U-Boat Codes, 1939–1943* (1992); and F.H. Hinsley and Alan Stripp (eds.), *Codebreakers: The Inside Story of Bletchley Park* (1994).

INDEX

A

Aeneas Tacticus, 51
Alberti, Leon Battista, 52
American Standard Code for
    Information Interchange
    (ASCII), 3–4
Augustus Caesar, 52

B

binary-coded decimal (BCD)
    form, 4
block and stream ciphers,
    39–40, 69

C

Caesar cipher, 17–18
Caesar, Julius, 17–18, 52
credit card, "smart," 13–14
cryptanalysis
    overview of and basic
        principles, 41–46
    types of, 46–49
cryptography
    overview of, 1–2
    codes, ciphers, and
        authentication, 2–8
    for commercial and private
        uses, 8–14, 48
cryptosecurity, 7, 25, 37, 38

D

della Porta, Giambattista, 53
Diffie, Whitfield, 31–32,
    33, 34
digest, 37–39

E

e-commerce, 8–10, 11–13, 73
electronic cryptography,
    modern, 63–64
    Advanced Encryption
        Standard (AES), 4, 14,
        63, 73
    Data Encryption Standard
        (DES), 4, 14, 40, 63, 64,
        68–73
    and electronics, 64–67, 68
Enigma machine, 56, 59, 60,
    61, 62
error propagation, 40

F

Feistel ciphers, 71
Fibonacci sequence, 65, 67–68
fractionation system, 28–29, 55
Friedman, Elizebeth, 27–28
Friedman, William F., 25,
    27–28, 61

G

Greeks, as early cryptographers, 38, 51

H

Hagelin M-209, 57–58
Hebern, Edward H., 55–56
Hellman, Martin, 31–32, 33, 34

I

identity theft, 12
Index of Coincidence and Its Application in Cryptography, The, 28

J

Japanese rotor machines, 61–62, 72

K

Kasiski, Friedrich, 22, 25, 47
Klaka-shandī, al-, 52

L

Lucifer algorithm, 68–69, 71

M

manual and mechanical cryptography, early, 50–51
    first systems, 51–54
    World Wars I and II, 25, 27–29, 41, 43–44, 50–51, 53, 54–62, 63, 64, 72
Mauborgne, Joseph, 25
Midway, Battle of, 41

O

onetime key, 7, 18, 25, 40, 54
On the Defense of Fortifications, 51

P

Painvin, Georges, 29
personal identity number (PIN), 13–14
pin-and-lug machines, 57–58, 60, 66
Playfair ciphers, 18–20, 39, 40
Polybius, 51
prime numbers, 25, 34, 35, 36, 38, 57
product ciphers, 28–29, 55, 69, 72
public-key cryptography, 33–35, 64

R

rail fence cipher, 15–16
Rejewski, Marian, 59
Rejewski's Bomba, 59
Rijndael program, 73
rotor cipher machines, 40, 50, 55–62, 63, 64, 72
route ciphers, 15–17
RSA (Rivest-Shamir-Adleman) encryption, 36–40, 48

S

scytale, 51
secret-sharing, 35–36
Shannon, Claude, 25
single-key cryptography, 25,
    30–31, 34, 39, 44, 47, 48,
    49, 72
substitution ciphers, 15, 17–26,
    30, 44, 45, 46, 51, 52, 54, 55,
    57, 64, 71, 72

T

Traicté de chiffres, 53–54
transposition ciphers, 15–17, 28
Trattati in cifra, 52–53
Turing, Alan, 59–60

Turing's Bombe, 59–60
two-key cryptography, 30, 31–39,
    47, 48, 49

U

U.S. Army Signal Corps, 25, 53, 55

V

Vernam-Vigenère ciphers, 24–26,
    40, 57, 58, 60
Vigenère ciphers, 20–24, 47, 54

Z

Zimmermann telegram, 41, 43–44